1001 IDEAS FOR
WINDOWS

P9-ELX-694

1001 IDEAS FOR WINDOWS

Anne Justin

CREATIVE
HOMEOWNER®

First published in North America in 2004 by

CREATIVE
HOMEOWNER®

Creative Homeowner® is a registered trademark of Federal Marketing Corp.

Copyright © 2004 Marshall Editions
All rights reserved

A Marshall Edition
Conceived, edited, and designed by Marshall Editions
The Old Brewery
6 Blundell Street
London N7 9BH
U.K.
www.quarto.com

Copyright under International, Pan American, and Universal Copyright Conventions. All rights reserved. No part of this book may be reproduced or transmitted in any form or by any means, electronic or mechanical, including photocopying, recording, or by any information storage-and-retrieval system, without written permission from the copyright holder.

ISBN 1 58011 224 2
Library of Congress Catalog Number 2004103757

Current printing (last digit)
10 9 8 7 6 5 4

Originated in Singapore by Chroma Graphics
Printed and bound in China

Author: Anne Justin
Illustrator: Elsa Godfry
Photography pp.100–111: Wolf Marloh
Design: Ivo Marloh, Roger Christian
Commissioning Editor: Claudia Martin
Editor: Sharon Hynes
Indexer: Judith Wardman
Production: Nikki Ingram and Anna Pauletti

CREATIVE HOMEOWNER
A Division of Federal Marketing Corp.
24 Park Way
Upper Saddle River, NJ 07458

www.creativehomeowner.com

Contents

Introduction

Windows are where the indoors meets the outdoors. By letting in light and fresh air, they literally make rooms livable; by revealing views of the world outside, they create a sense of space and foster a connection with nature. In any interior, windows are natural focal points. How they are treated has a great impact on the character, mood, and style of a room.

Opposite Puddled curtains with a contrasting hem panel on French windows. The pole is fixed well above the windows so as not to impede opening.

Above Honeycomb blinds make a light and breezy treatment. These have retractable cords.

From delicate sheer drapery to crisp, tailored blinds, from dressy swags to elaborate draperies with all the trimmings, the decorative potential of window treatments is enormous. There are hundreds of different approaches and combinations with which to experiment. Whatever your taste and budget, *1001 Ideas for Windows* offers all the options, both practical and stylistic, to enable you to choose the perfect treatment for any window in any location.

Windows come in all shapes and sizes, often reflecting the architectural character of your home. The first chapter, "Designing Windows," reviews all the different types of windows, from picture windows to bays, French doors to dormers, giving practical advice on how to tackle each specific style or format, as well as offering some more unusual ideas.

Subsequent chapters explore every conceivable window treatment, beginning with curtains (covering the basics of length, panel width, heading, and tying back) and proceeding through valances; cornices and lambrequins; swags and scarves; shades; and blinds and shutters. Accessories, such as tassels and fringes, and all the hardware options, such as decorative poles, clips, and finials, are also detailed. Fabrics are covered in a separate chapter, with a wide range of examples covering all the options from silks to cottons and sheers to brocades. With invaluable window treatment templates so you can experiment with mixing and matching the different options, and a detailed practical

Below Transparent blinds are overhung by Roman shades for maximum light control.

Bottom A sheer roller shade and flimsy floral curtains soften the light in this pretty and feminine bedroom.

checklist, this sourcebook provides a richly comprehensive guide to decorating windows with style.

Before you begin to dip into the following pages, it is worth taking the time to think about a few basic issues. In terms of style, the main variables to consider include color, pattern, and texture, as revealed in your choice of fabric, along with whether to opt for a traditional, classic, or modern approach. You might go for a sympathetic complement to your existing decor, such as period-style swags in a historic setting, or clean-lined blinds in a contemporary space; or choose a bold contrast for a signature statement. Additions such as holdbacks, cornices, and valances provide decorative flourishes that broaden the scope still further.

But style is only part of the story. Window treatments are not exclusively about window dressing: practical issues also have a role to play. Thinking about the quality of light, scale and proportion, and issues concerning privacy and security, is also an important part of the whole decision-making process.

Quality of light

One of the main functions of the window is to let in light. Natural light is very appealing. Unlike artificial light, it is not uniform, but changes constantly in strength and color throughout the day and from season to season. These subtle variations bring vitality to the interior and put us in touch with the natural world.

All window treatments modify light in some way: heavy, lined draperies block it completely; translucent sheers soften and diffuse it; slatted blinds create moody patterns of light and shade. Before you choose a treatment, think about the quality of light that you are trying to achieve.

Where light levels are low or in rooms with poor aspects, treatments that frame the window but do not obscure it may be preferable. Sunlight is not always welcome, however. In hot climates, where light is strong and there is a risk of overheating, you may need to block out the sun's glare at critical times of the day. Combinations of draperies and shades, or draperies and sheers, can provide the best of both worlds, filtering light in an interesting way without screening it completely.

Personal preference may also dictate choice. Some people like to wake up with the sun; others can sleep soundly only if light is blacked out completely. Interlined draperies are an effective way of excluding light; you can also purchase blackout fabric for shades in order to get the same effect.

Framing the view

Window treatments act as decorative surrounds for what a window reveals. A truly stunning view across open countryside or the sea needs little in

Above Shutters made of white-painted hardwood blend in with the casual decor and filter the light in an evocative way.

the way of embellishment. But many views, particularly in urban areas, are less desirable. Treatments that overhang the window, such as swags or full draperies with valances, cornices, or lambrequins, are useful ways of excluding unwelcome views. The traditional standby of the lace or sheer curtain allows light through while maintaining privacy.

If windows provide views out, they also allow others to see in. A lighted window at night-time is an invitation for the curious passerby. Window treatments provide essential screening from prying eyes, encourage a feeling of intimacy, and serve as an important

Above A subtle combination of color and pattern creates a warm, cozy effect. The draperies are trimmed with braid on their leading edges.

Traditionally, window treatments have been one of the most significant applications of soft furnishing in the interior—and the scope of suitable fabrics is correspondingly wide. More recently, however, blinds and shutters in a range of different materials, including metal and wood, have also formed an increasingly important part of the repertoire.

The prominence of the window as a feature means that your choice of color will pack an extra punch. Window treatments can be designed to blend in with decorative choices elsewhere in the room, repeating colors used on the walls, furniture, or flooring for a coordinated look. Alternatively, you may wish to opt for a strong accent or contrast that introduces a jolt of color to an otherwise muted scheme. Historical palettes are widely available if your aim is to reproduce an authentic look. One of the most satisfying ways of using color at the window is to play with the complementary shades—such as red with green, or blue with yellow—choosing one color as the dominant theme and trimming or accenting it with its complementary partner.

security measure at a time of day when we tend to feel most vulnerable. How much privacy you require will depend on the location of the window and the degree to which it is overlooked by neighboring properties or adjacent streets.

Color, pattern, and texture

As a vehicle for decoration, window treatments offer the opportunity to experiment with color, pattern, and texture. More often than not, these elements tend to be expressed in the form of a specific choice of fabric.

Color can also help to mediate the effect of natural light. Shades such as yellows, golds, pinks, and earthy reds add a warming note in a room that receives little direct light; cool blues and neutrals are airy, restful, and light-enhancing. Richer shades create an immediate feeling of coziness.

Pattern is equally important. Because pattern is all about repetition, it has an intrinsic rhythm and movement that can bring immense vitality to the interior. From traditional to contemporary, country-casual to city-smart, there are many designs from

which to choose. Trailing or branching patterns work better in window treatments where the fabric is gathered or folded; geometric or large-scale motifs are preferable where the fabric will be displayed flat, as in the case of shades. As with color, a window treatment can provide the means to coordinate patterns throughout the room for a rich, layered effect; or display a pattern as a focal point, adding vital decorative interest.

Texture invites touch. Fabric weight, pile, and weave, as well as the type of fiber, provide subtle interest

Below left Floor-length button-tab curtains in a geometric print lend richness to the muted color scheme.

Below right Braiding makes a graphic contrast to thick velvet draperies suspended from rings in this daringly patterned room.

that lends depth of character. Heavy furnishing fabrics such as velvet and damask inject a sense of luxury, while delicate sheers have a sensual appeal. Crisp cotton, shimmering silk, and raw linen all have their own characteristics which add further dimensions to decorative choice.

Proportion and design

There are countless ways in which a window treatment can be used to correct basic deficiencies of proportion and scale, not merely of windows but also of the room itself. Height can be lessened by dropping a valance or cornice below the top of the window; height can be added by adopting the reverse strategy. Narrow windows can be visually widened by extending the curtains beyond the frame to either side; wide windows can be narrowed by curtains that overhang the glass.

Windows not only come in different shapes and sizes, they also vary in their means of operation: some slide up and down or side to side; some open inward or outward; others may not open at all. A window treatment must not only suit the proportion and style of window but should also allow clear access to it.

Finding inspiration

Throughout history, window treatments have followed trends not only in other forms of interior furnishing but also in styles of dress. Empire-style window drapery, tied back high on the window frame, echoes the high-waisted silhouette fashionable in women's dress of the early 19th century. Late 19th-century windows, hung with layers of richly trimmed draperies and shades, similarly follow the elaborate clothing styles of the period. The pared-down look of contemporary shades and blinds finds its complement in the relative simplicity of modern dress. But interior fashions, no less than clothing styles, are always ripe for revival. Many traditional features, such as cornices and lambrequins, have seen a comeback in recent years; historical designs still provide a wealth of inspiration for distinctive treatments.

Studying the original illustrations in the historical picture galleries throughout this book will give you ideas for period-style effects. The photo galleries provide contemporary interpretations of some of these classic designs, as well as modern solutions for creative inspiration.

Opposite top and bottom These pretty French door treatments date from the late 19th century. The upper and lower portions of the window are individually screened with lace panels.

Above Goblet-pleat headings add a note of refinement. Draperies for the arched window follow the shape of the curve.

Right These early 19th-century French illustrations display fanciful treatments for arched windows with elaborate scarves looped over poles.

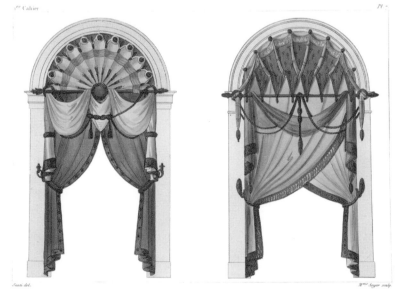

Designing Windows

When it comes to deciding which window treatment to choose, the starting point is the window itself. Windows come in a wide range of shapes, sizes, and styles—some are straightforward to cover; others are more problematic. Many solutions to the more challenging types of window will actually enhance their overall style and character.

Window shape and size have an obvious impact on the choice of treatment. Regular rectilinear shapes are much easier to cover than shapes that are angled or curved. Similarly, standard sizes are economical to treat because you have access to a wide range of ready-made options, from curtains and draperies to shades and blinds. Windows in odd sizes need more consideration.

Very small windows can easily be overwhelmed by a fussy treatment and often look best with simple shades or blinds. At the other end of the scale, very large windows can be expensive to cover with fabric, and draperies may prove heavy and unwieldy to operate. While most windows require some form of treatment, period-style windows, with fine muntins, are features in their own right and should be left exposed to view or minimally covered wherever possible.

Positioning is another factor to consider. Corner windows, high windows, and roof windows all require specific solutions. Recessed windows, such as dormers and some casements, along with bay and bow windows, which create their own alcoves, also need careful thought.

In practical terms, a window treatment should be designed so that it does not interfere with the way that a window opens. This is particularly important for French doors, which lead onto outdoor areas.

This striking combination of curtains and blinds offers dramatic style as well as flexible light control.

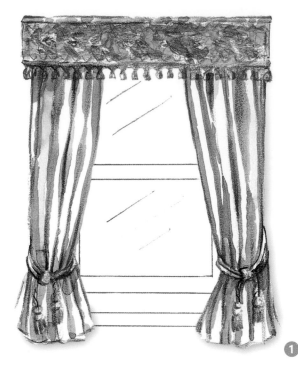

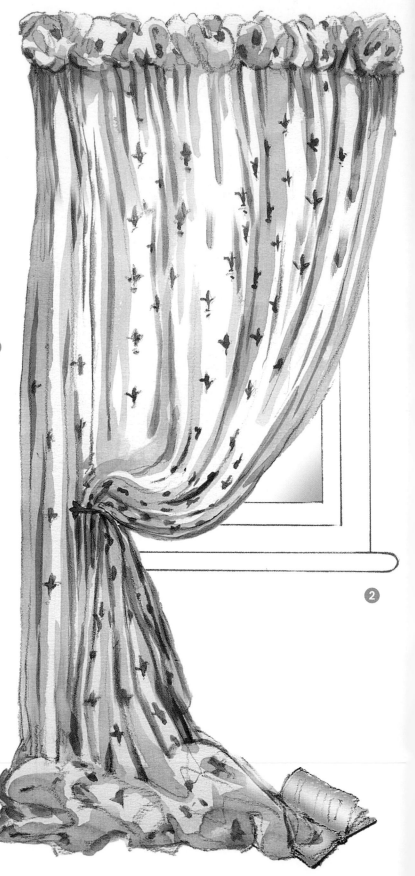

The double-hung window is a traditional window type that consists of two sashes, at least one of which slides up or down over the other. When both sashes are operable, ventilation is maximized. Raising the lower sash and lowering the upper sash allows cool air to come in below while warm escapes at the top. These windows are very common and easy to decorate due to their regular shape. The main practical consideration is to provide clear access for opening the window.

1   Sill-length velvet curtains, held back by tasseled ropes, with a tapestry-covered box cornice

2   Puddled sheer with puffed rod-pocket heading

3   Tailored fabric valance hung over a Roman shade

4   Sheer with a bead-trimmed foldover heading

5   Gathered valance and tiebacks over a roller shade

6   Floor-length tab-top curtains hung from a rustic pole

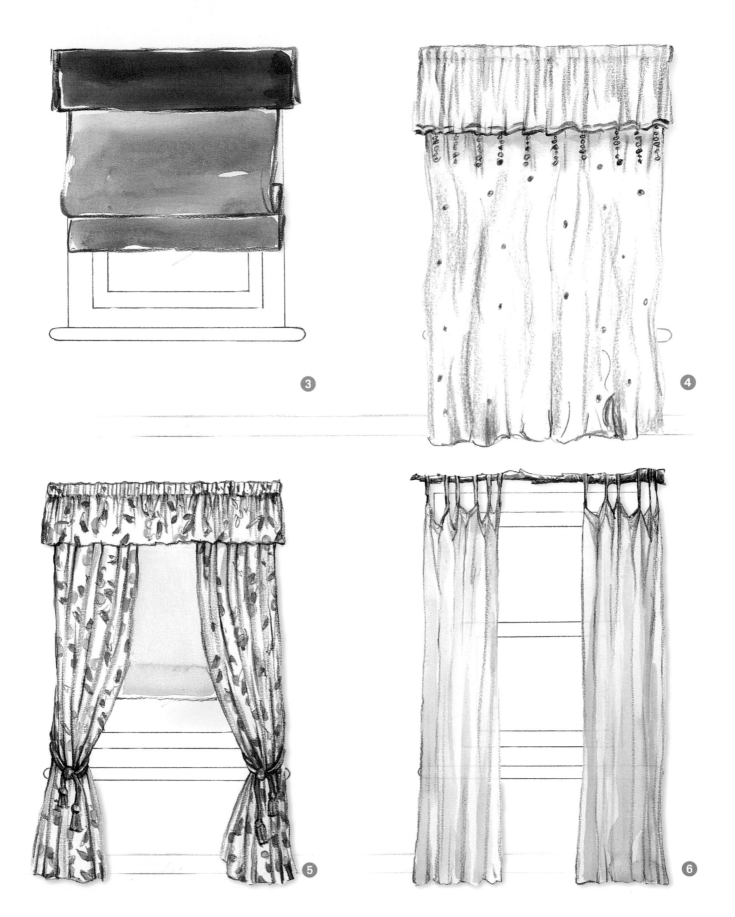

The picture window offers an expansive view largely uninterrupted by individual panes or frames. Suitable treatments range from full formal draperies topped with a valance to affordable shades.

1 Rope-trimmed draperies with a rope-loop heading

2 Puddled silk curtains with a simple foldover heading

3 A swagged valance over heavy draperies

4 A tailed balloon shade with a goblet-pleat heading

5 Heavy brocade draperies and a scalloped cornice

6 A roller shade under a contrasting smocked valance

3

4

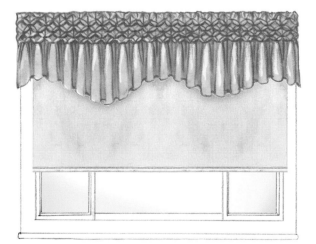

5

6

Bays form angled recesses, whereas bows form curved ones. Curtains may be hung outside the recess, with shades or blinds used to cover individual windows. Alternatively, use curved or angled tracks or rods to hang panels directly on the window frames.

1 A velvet pleated valance and floor-length draperies

2 A pennant valance over matching roller shades

3 Rosette-trimmed shades with cotton draperies outside the recess

4 "Italian-strung" curtains with a puffed rod-pocket heading

5 Double-tracked sill-length draperies in contrasting fabrics

6 Vinyl miniblinds with Roman shades

1

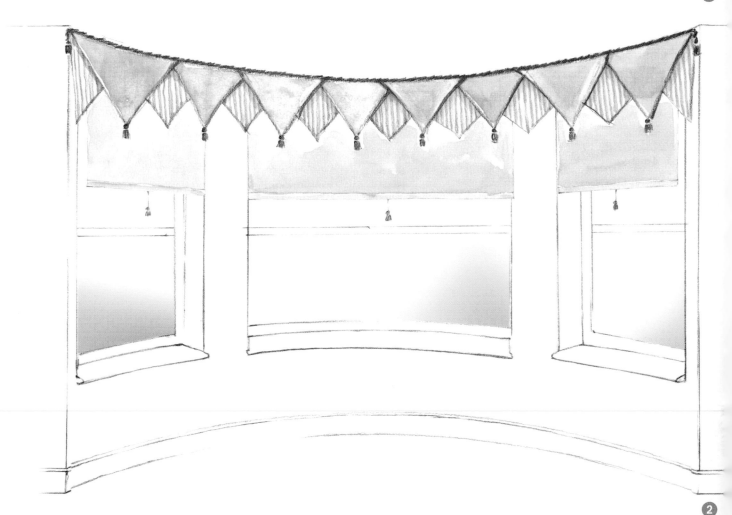

2

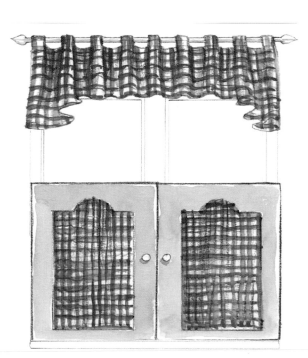

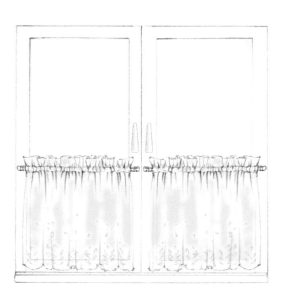

One of the oldest window types, casements are hinged vertically and open either inward or outward. The treatment you choose should not interfere with the way the window opens. When a casement is recessed, curtains can be hung from a rod on the outer wall.

1   A Roman shade with a light knotted scarf

2   Lace café curtains on individual poles

3   Fabric-insert café shutters and a matching tab-top valance

4   Puddled curtains with a double-swagged valance

5   Pencil-pleat curtains with metal holdbacks and pole

6   Sill-length tented tiebacks with a contrasting lining

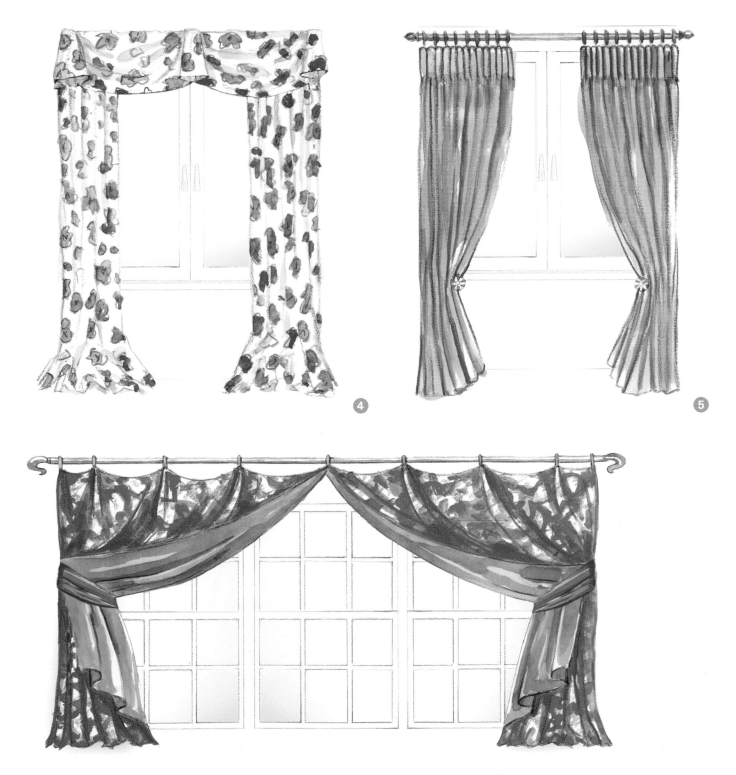

Any treatment for French doors or sliding doors must allow easy passage. One solution is to suspend curtains high above the frame and extend the track or rod clear of it on either side so that the fabric does not get caught in the doors. Alternatively, the curtains themselves may be stationary, with lace panels, sheers, or blinds installed on the doors.

1 Puddled silk curtains with a toning foldover heading and tiebacks

2 Floor-length print curtains with a contrasting heading

3 Casual floor-length curtains with individual jute Roman shades

4 A bow-tied valance and floor-length draperies

5 Fabric Roman shades

6 An asymmetric curtain with tabbed heading and fabric tieback

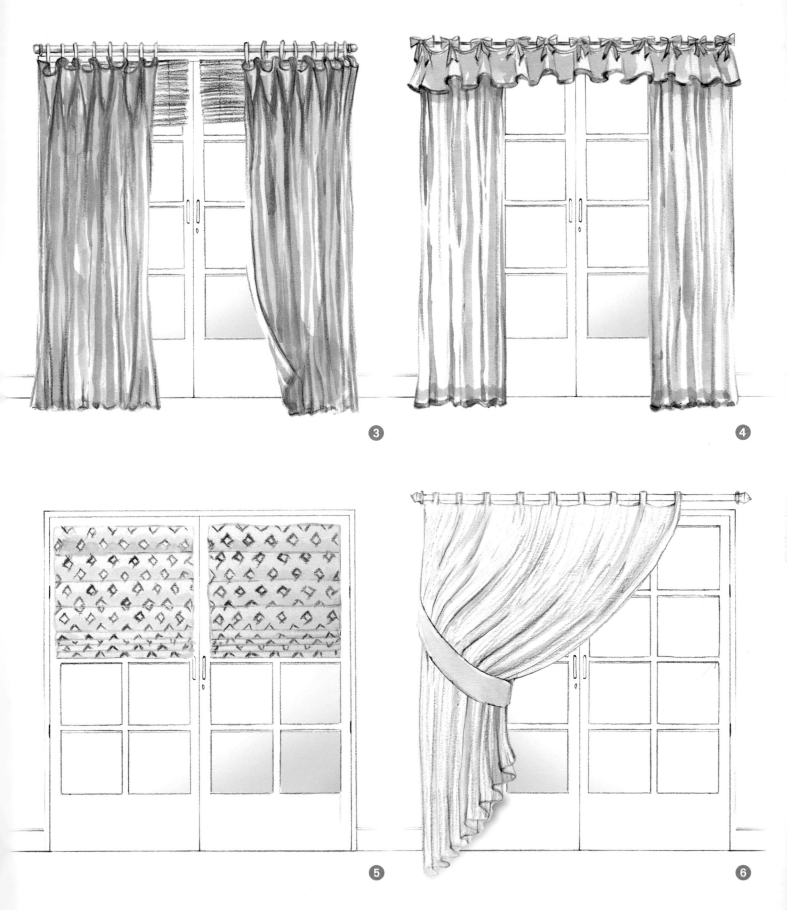

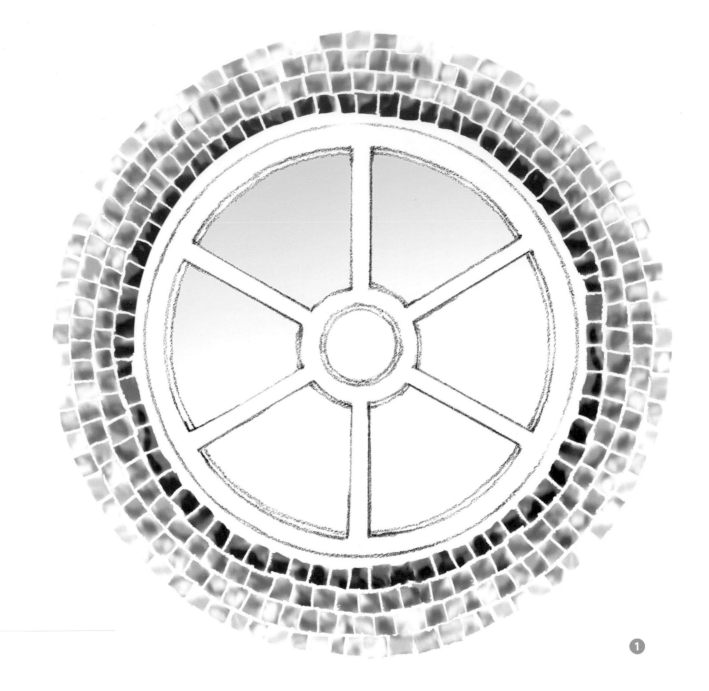

1

Round windows are graceful architectural features and do not need much in the way of covering, if anything. If you would like to dress the window for privacy or security, treatments that gather the fabric into billows or curves will complement the window shape.

1   A fading circle of mosaic tiles

2   A floor-length silk scarf over a mid-window pole

3   Bright paint highlighting the unusual window shape

4   A sheer circular curtain for complete privacy

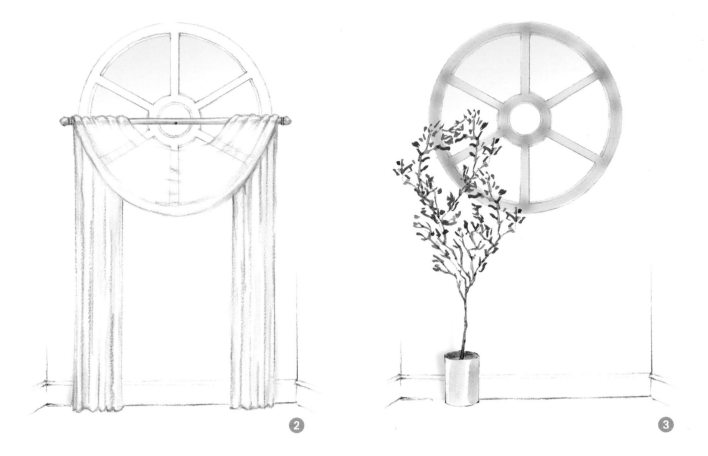

2

3

4

Corner windows can be problematic if there is little margin in the corner for each window to be dressed as a separate unit. For unified effects, angled corner rods are available. Alternatively, individual blinds or shades can be mounted inside the frames.

1 A looped-and-knotted muslin scarf across both windows

2 Tab-topped valances

3 Formal swag and jabots with contrasting border panels

4 Balloon shades

5 Matchstick blinds

6 Asymmetric swag and jabots

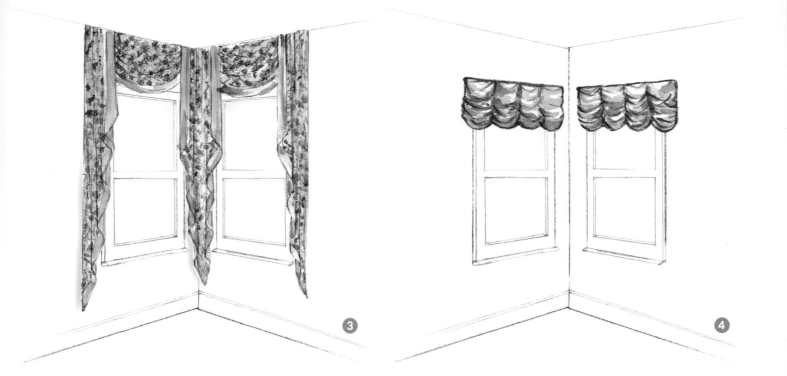

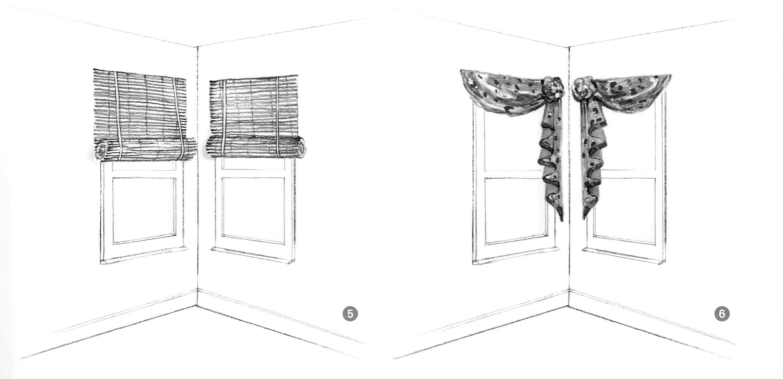

These windows are often so decorative that it is a pity to cover them. Leaving the arched, pointed, or angled top clear and covering only the lower, rectangular section of the window is a good option for light control and privacy.

1 Pierced curtains over the lower windows only

2 Fabric panels with gathered draperies

3 A sheer with a braided heading

4 Silk loop-tops below the arch

5 Dramatic custom curtain

6 A complex swag and jabot treatment

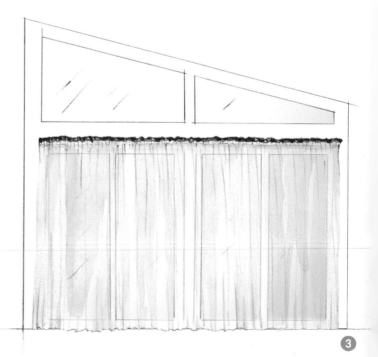

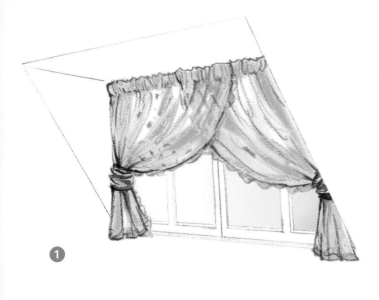

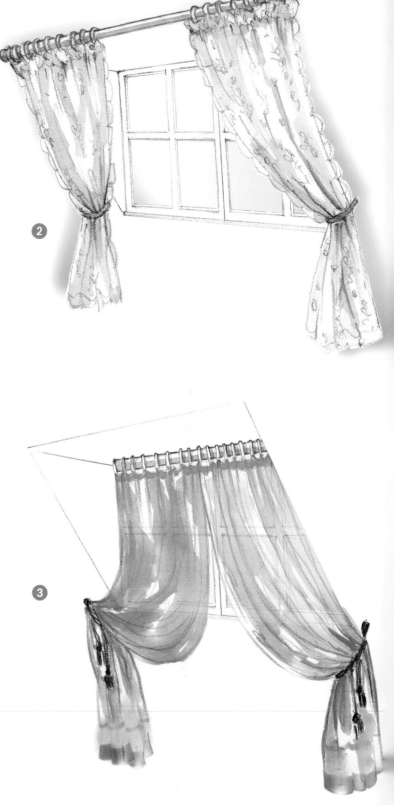

Dormer windows, which are set within a recess projecting from the sloping plane of the roof, often do not have enough wall space at either side to allow for standard curtains. Hinged or swivel rods are one solution. Another is to suspend the curtain outside the recess. Or, if you don't mind sacrificing a little light, short curtains can be fixed to the frame and softly pulled back to either side.

1 Short crossover tiebacks fixed to the frame

2 Lace panels hanging outside the recess and tied back to the wall

3 Sheers fixed to the window frame but tied to the outer wall

4 A swag and jabot treatment with rosettes

5 Rod-pocket tiebacks on swivel rods

6 Ring-headed draperies, held back to the wall by a pole

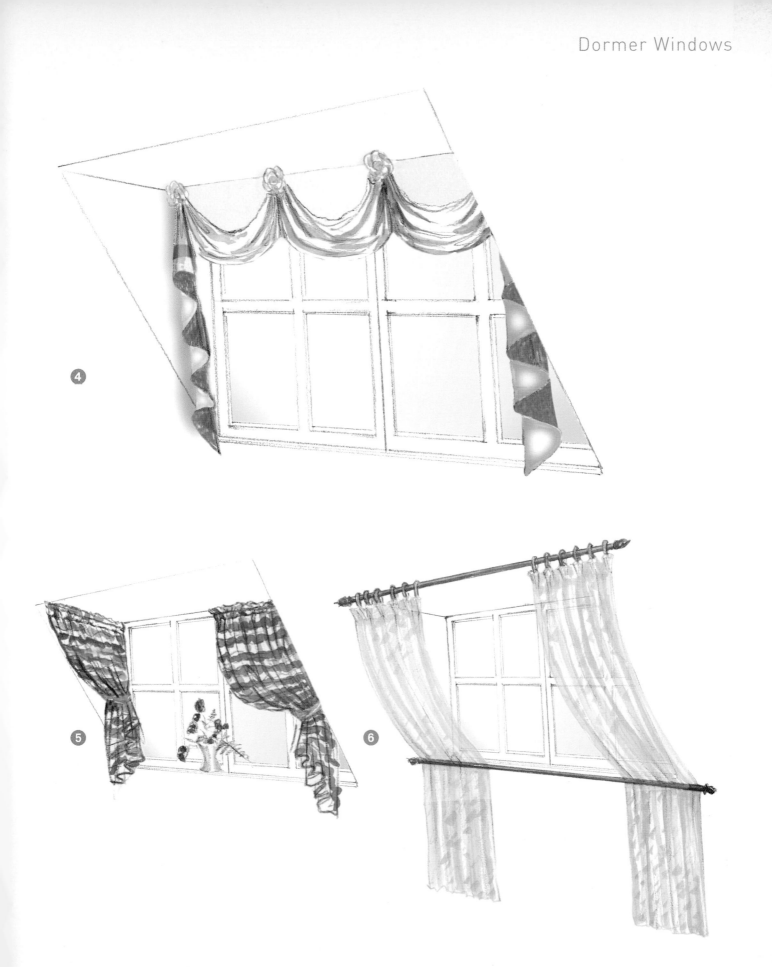

Skylights are most dramatic when left uncovered, but you will sometimes need to screen strong sunlight in some way. Shades are a common solution as they can be fixed to the frame. Other problem windows include jalousies, with their horizontal glass louvers; windows with unusual proportions; and windows set too close to the ceiling to leave room for a track or rod.

1 Ceiling-mounted clips and a bow-tied heading

2 A tear-drop valance to correct the window's proportions

3 A roller shade

4 A "sail" shade, held back by ropes and rings

5 Individual roller shades with a cornice box

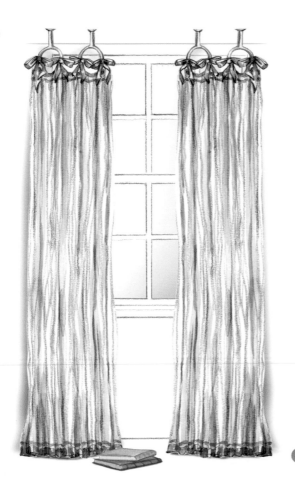

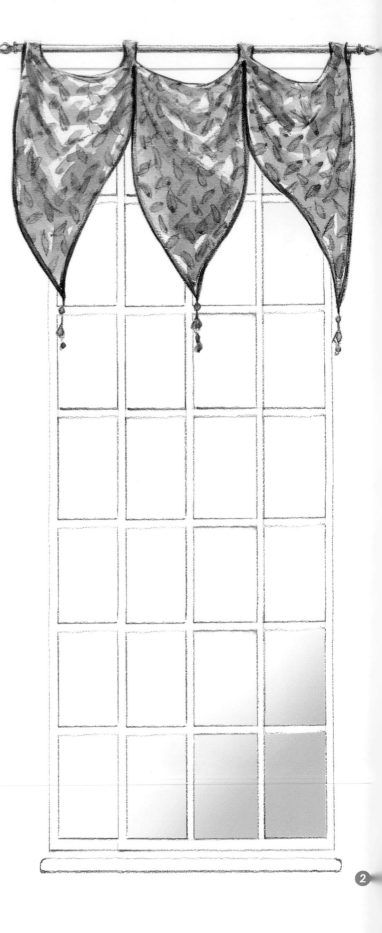

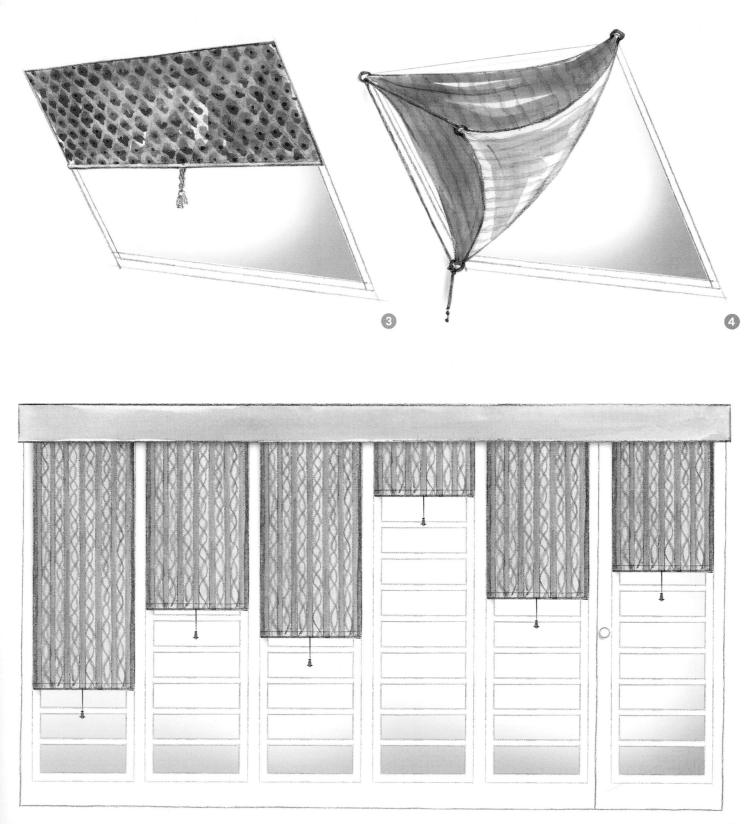

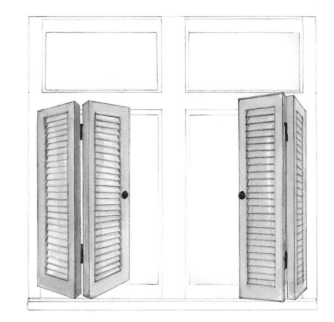

Transoms and sidelights are portions of clear window set above or beside doors or other windows. These feature windows can often be treated most effectively by leaving them without covering. If you are concerned about security or privacy, plain glass can be replaced by opaque or colored glass, or covered with lace or sheer panels. Alternatively, choose a treatment, such as individual blinds or curtains, that spotlights, rather than obscures, the feature.

1 Floor-length draperies with a sheer panel over the transoms

2 Painted shutters below the transoms

3 Individual printed Roman shades

4 A fabric Venetian blind covering the central panel only

5 Individual curtains made from strings of glass beads

6 A single Roman shade with undressed sidelights

Curtains and Draperies

Curtains and draperies are by far the most popular option for dressing windows. Fabric, either gathered or hung in panels, adds a softening element to the interior and provides the opportunity to display pattern and color, either in contrast to other furnishings or coordinated with them.

A sheer sill-length curtain with a rod-pocket heading has a scalloped hem and daisy embroidery.

Curtain style is largely a function of the type of heading; in turn, the heading will determine the width of the curtain and how much fabric will be required. Simple headings include the rod pocket (where a rod is inserted into a fabric pocket at the top of the curtain) and ties or tab tops that loop over a pole. Gathered headings, for which fabric is shirred by means of a corded strip sewn on the reverse, are soft and pretty. Pleated headings have a more formal, tailored appearance.

Another important variable is length. Depending on the effect you want to create, as well as more practical matters, you can choose between sill-length, below-sill length, floor-length, and trailing or "puddled." Shorter curtains suit horizontal windows; they are also more practical if windows are frequently opened, or if there is a radiator beneath the window that should not be blocked. Longer draperies have a more formal, traditional appearance. Because they are necessarily heavier, they must be easy to operate. Puddled curtains are theatrical and luxurious but should be avoided in areas where they might cause people to trip. Other types include café curtains, which cover the lower half of the window, and stationary panels, which do not close.

Lining improves the shape of the curtain; interlining blocks light and provides insulation against heat-loss and sound. Contrasting lining adds a subtle tone to the facing pattern when the light shines through. Shaped or trimmed hems, along with tying back, provide yet more decorative options.

Choice of heading goes a long way towards defining the style of the curtain. There are a huge range of options, from soft gathered styles to more formal tailored versions. A heading should be chosen with reference to the type of fabric as well as its pattern. Lightweight sheers suit informal gathered or shirred styles; heavier, more textured fabrics lend themselves to the crisp detail of pleating.

1 A soft foldover heading accentuating the sensual quality of silk

2 A neat button-tab heading in a contrasting pattern accenting plain curtains

3 Supremely elegant French pleats keep fabric hanging in straight columns

4 Pretty ties suspending lightweight sheer curtains for an airy effect

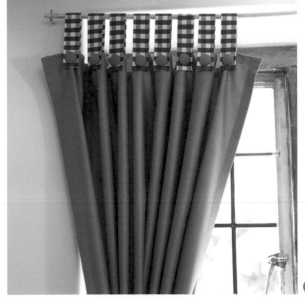

3

4

Lengths, hems, and how curtains are tied back are all important stylistic variables. Sill- or below-sill lengths are simple, neat, and practical, particularly for kitchens and bathrooms. At the opposite extreme, puddled draperies that trail on the floor are deeply luxurious. Tying back is not simply a practical means of securing fabric: it also affects the silhouette and apparent fullness of the curtain, as well as determining how much light a room receives.

1 Double-tracked curtains in fresh and breezy fabrics

2 Double-layered sheer curtain in contrasting colors, informally looped up over a decorative rod

3 Tall windows in a period setting accentuated by dramatic puddled velvet draperies

4 Contrasting-colored hems adding graphic definition to columns of floor-length draperies

1

2

3

4

5

As the 19th century drew to a close, interior furnishings became increasingly lighter and less detailed. Simple curtains hung from poles replaced elaborate treatments with valances and all the trimmings. By the 1920s, the curves of Art Deco were shaping window treatments.

6

1 A late 19th-century European design in the Aesthetic Movement style

2 Print of a 1920s Art Deco bedroom

3 A late 19th-century watercolor of a French interior with tiebacks

4 A 1903 bedroom interior, designed by George Logan, a member of the Glasgow Mackintosh circle

5 The stylized curvilinear forms of Art Deco

6 An 1890s European bathroom design

2

Like many periods, the 1950s were both forward- and backward-looking. Modernity came in the form of geometric prints; nostalgia was reflected in the vogue for Regency-style decoration.

1 Simple draperies in a vivid yellow held in position by Regency-style holdbacks

2 A bold geometric pattern

3 The pretty homemaker look: sheer gathered curtains with braid edging

4 Café curtains suspended over a shade

5 Pleated draperies featuring a dramatic geometric print

1

3

4

5

1

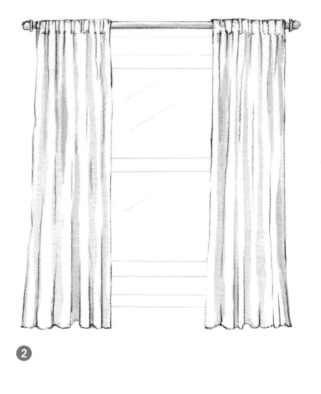

2

The options are endless when it comes to curtain-length, but there are some basic principles, both practical and stylistic, to keep in mind. Generally speaking, the longer the panel, the more formal the effect. Also bear in mind the style of the room, the positioning of the window, and its opening mechanism.

1 Sill-length curtains are the practical choice for a window in a recess or above furniture, or for one that is opened frequently.

2 For the ideal proportions, below-sill-length curtains should fall about 4 inches below the sill.

3 Floor-length draperies can be both formal and elegant in effect and should fall to about ½ inch above the floor.

4 For dramatic puddled curtains—which are not suitable for windows around which there will be a lot of traffic—add another 5–6 inches of fabric, which is to be arranged in poufs on the floor.

5 Casual half-length "café curtains" allow both natural light and privacy.

6 Tiered café curtains offer the informality of café curtains with the added option of complete privacy.

3

4

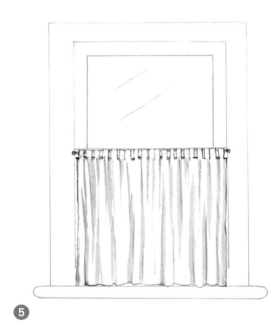

5

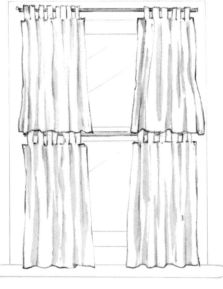

6

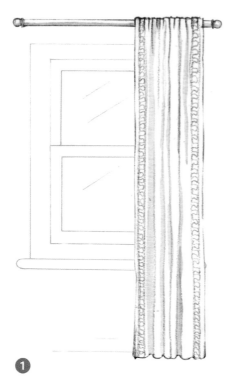

Choice of panel width depends on practical considerations, such as the positioning of the window and its opening mechanism, as well as the style you are trying to achieve.

1 A single panel can extend across the whole window or be purely decorative.

2 Two equal panels are the practical option for smaller windows.

④

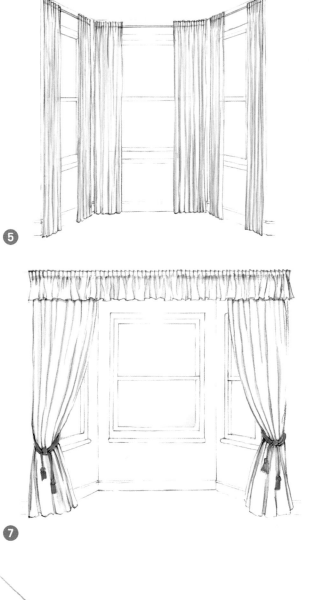

⑤

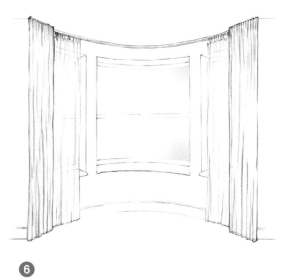

⑥

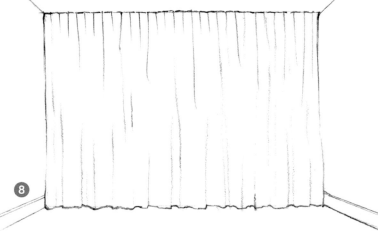

⑦

3 Three panels add interest to a wide window or two windows positioned close together.

4 Four panels are ideal for a bay or bow window.

5 Multiple panels give optimum versatility.

6 Double-tracked draperies work most effectively when the inner curtain is in a contrasting or sheer fabric.

7 A surprising space can be created with curtains running across the front of a window recess.

8 Cover a whole wall with draperies to create a feature and the illusion of a wide window.

⑧

51

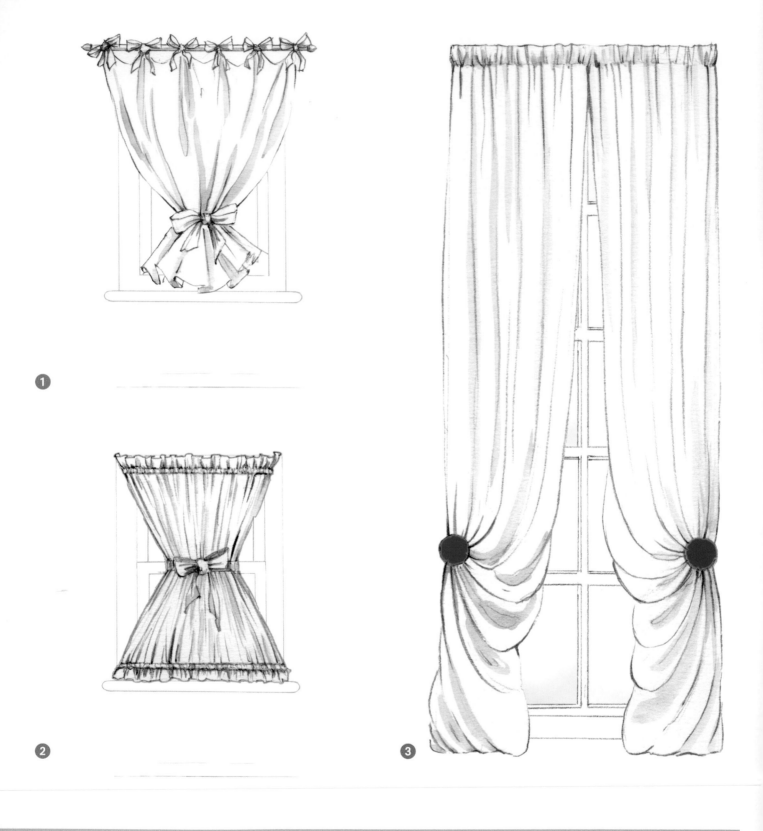

1 Central tieback

2 Rod pocket top and bottom

3 Elegant low ties

4 A single high tie

5 Tented tiebacks, with the inner lining on display

6 "Bishop's sleeve" draperies

7 Crossover tiebacks

④

⑤

⑥

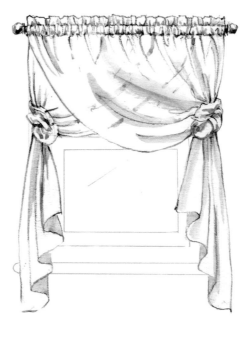

⑦

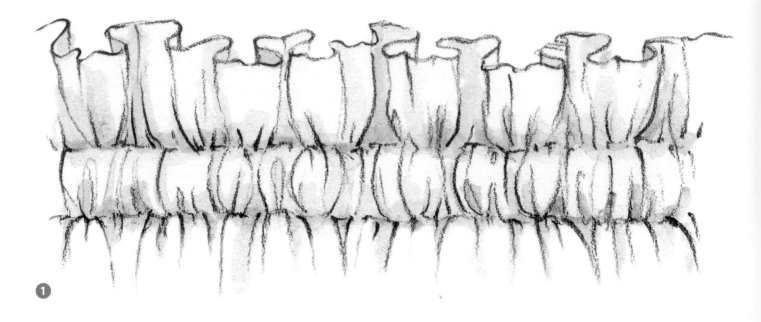

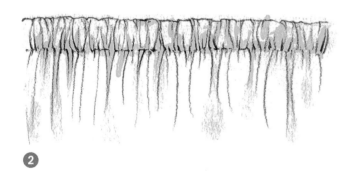

1

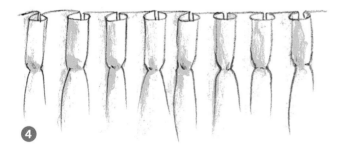

2

3

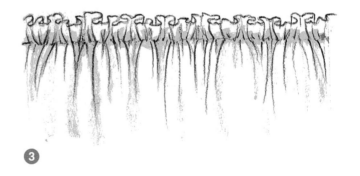

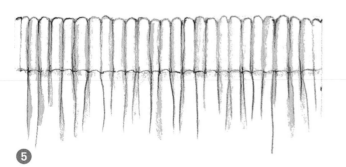

4

5

6

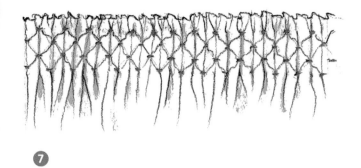

7

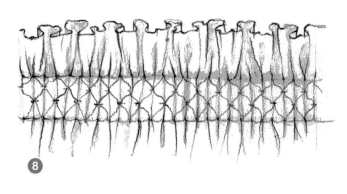

8

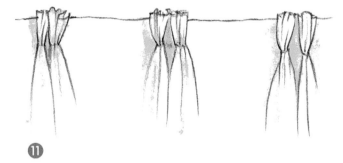

9

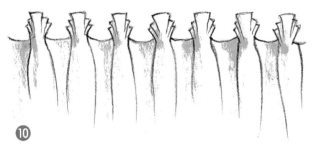

10

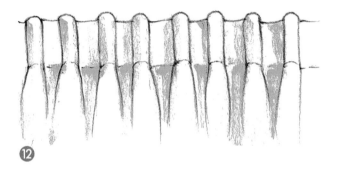

11

12

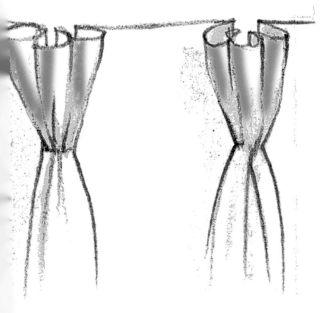

1	Ruffled rod pocket	7	Smocked
2	Plain rod pocket	8	Smocked with ruffle
3	Gathered	9	Box pleat
4	Goblet pleat	10	Fan pleat
5	Pencil pleat	11	Double French pleat
6	French, or triple, pleat	12	Cartridge pleat

1

2

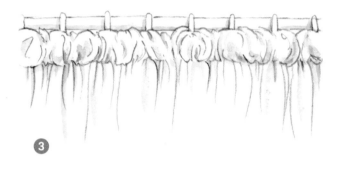

3

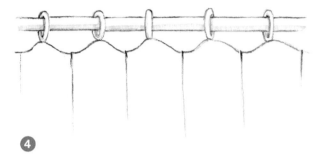

4

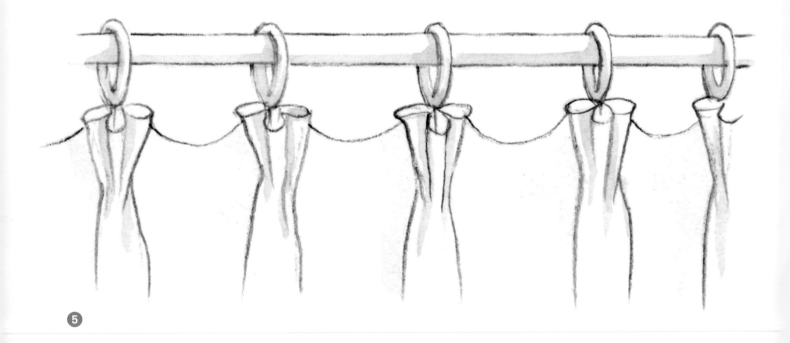

5

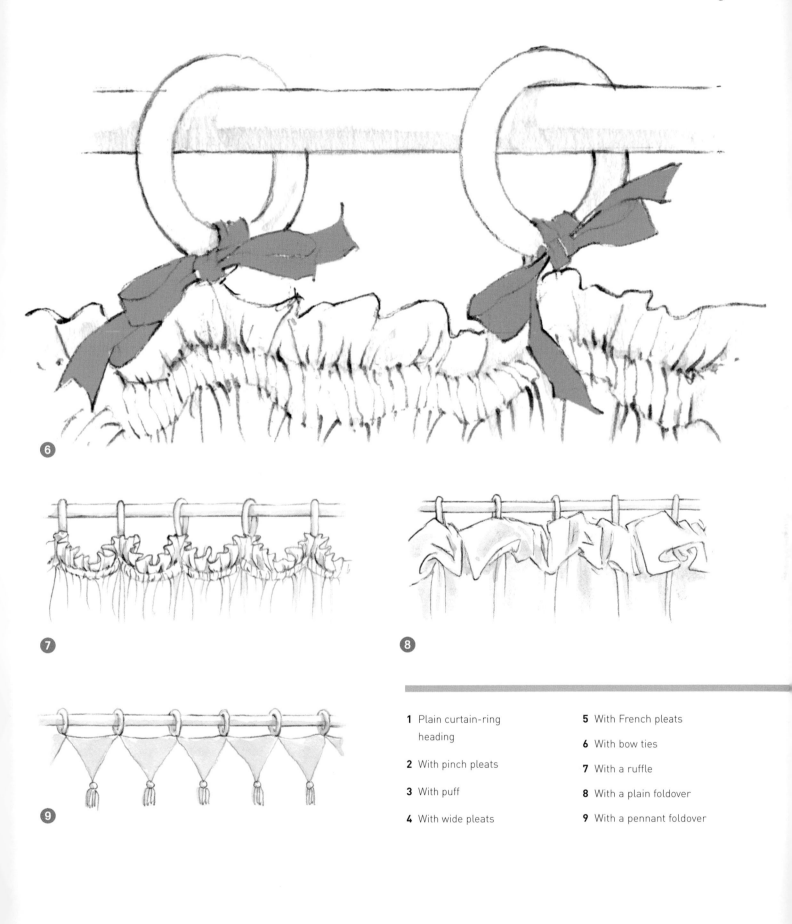

1 Plain curtain-ring heading

2 With pinch pleats

3 With puff

4 With wide pleats

5 With French pleats

6 With bow ties

7 With a ruffle

8 With a plain foldover

9 With a pennant foldover

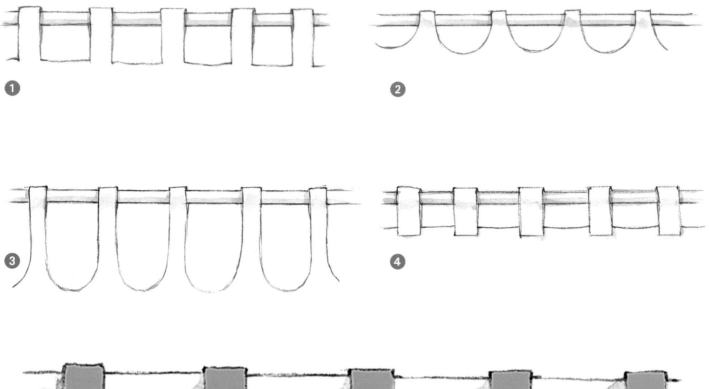

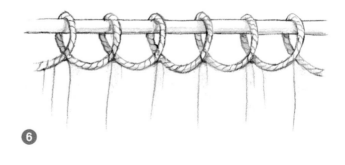

1 Loops	**7** Bow-tied loops
2 Loops with scallops	**8** Pierced
3 Loops with deep scallops	**9** Pierced with rope loops
4 Tabs	**10** Pierced with leather ties
5 Button tabs	**11** Rope loops on nails
6 Rope loops and edging	

7

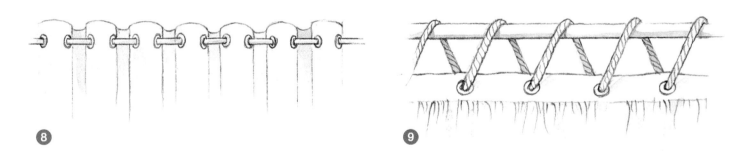

8

9

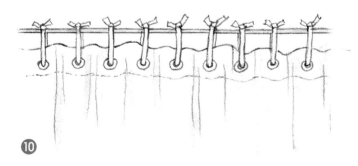

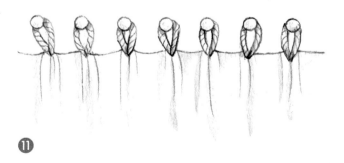

10

11

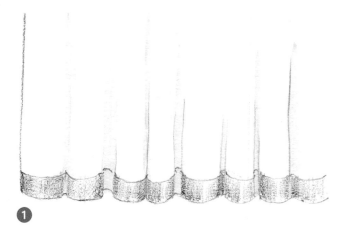

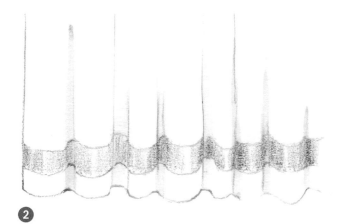

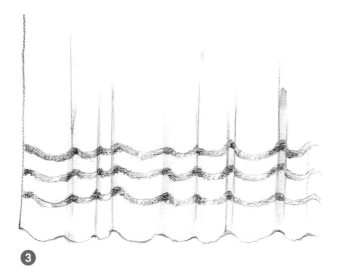

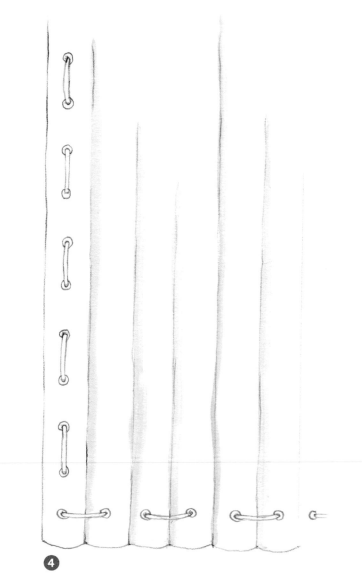

1	Contrasting border panel	**7**	Fringing
2	Inset border panel	**8**	Pleated ruffle
3	Triple rows of braid	**9**	Gathered with rosettes
4	Rope and eyelet border	**10**	Gathered with bows
5	Pintucks	**11**	Embroidered hem
6	Scalloped border panel		

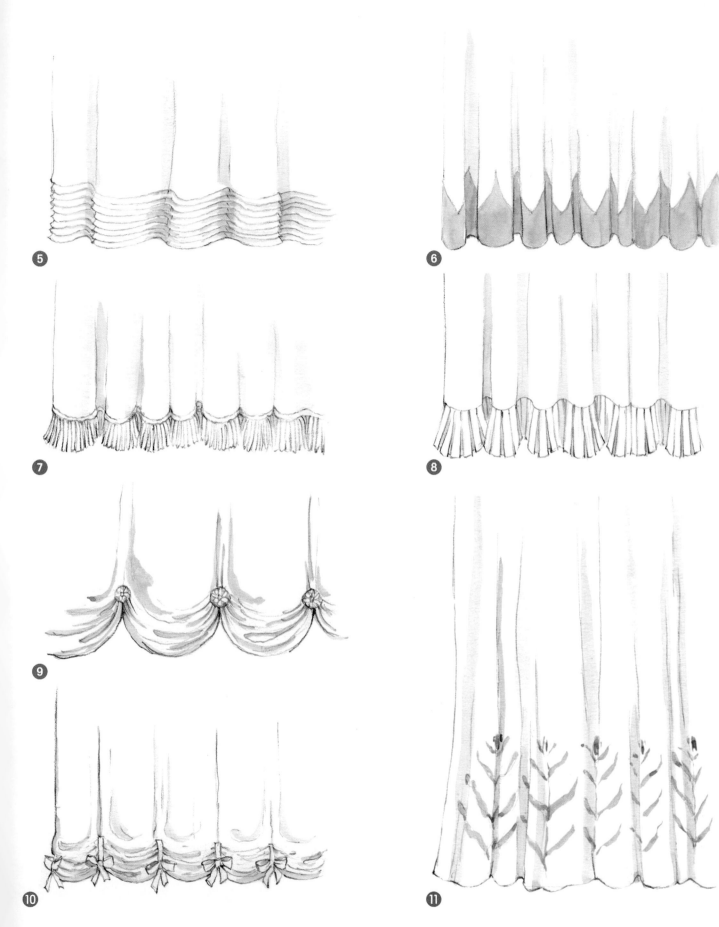

1

Before even introducing the additional elements of cornices, valances, swags, or shades, there are an infinite number of different combinations of length, panel width, heading, and hem with which to experiment. The addition of tiebacks can make the treatment fancy and ornamental or just plain casual.

2

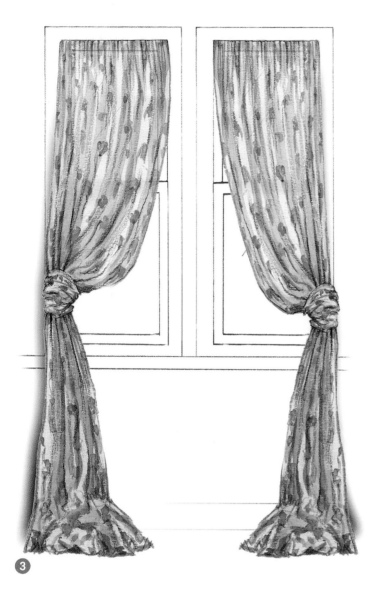

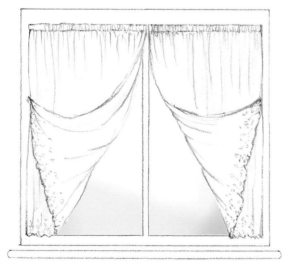

1 Café curtain with ruffled rod-pocket heading

2 Curtain suspended from rings with a contrasting
   hem panel

3 Puddled and knotted draperies with individual
   rod-pocket headings

4 A dramatically pinned-back sheer

5 Sill-length tied-back lace panels

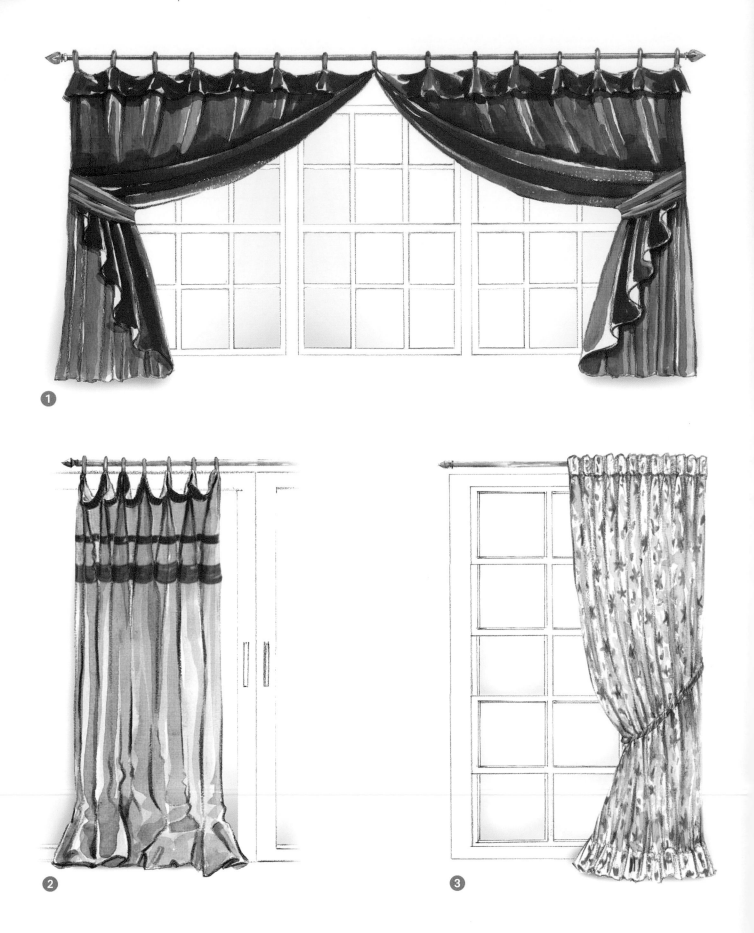

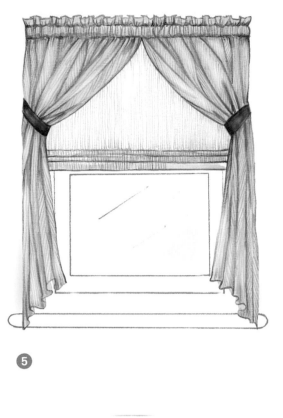

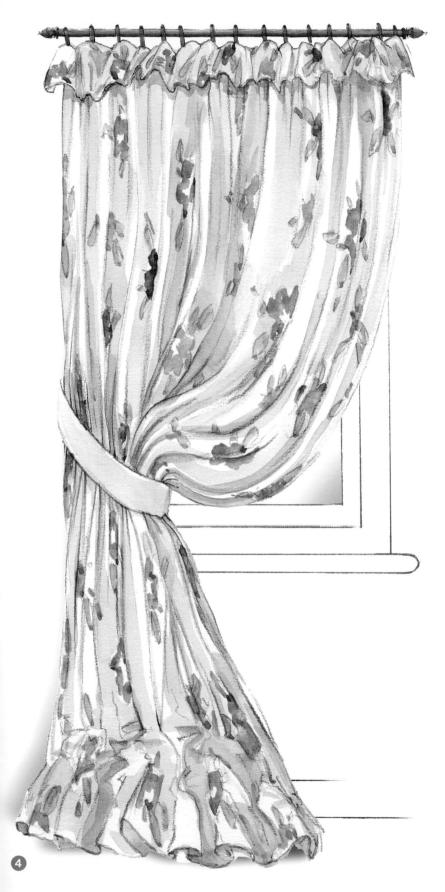

1 Below-sill-length curtains with a contrasting tented tieback and foldover heading

2 Puddled silk draperies with a scalloped curtain-ring heading and decorative braiding

3 Goblet-pleat heading, rope tieback, and a ruffled hem

4 Puddled curtain with a pouched tieback and foldover heading

5 Sill-length curtains with high ties and ruffled rod-pocket heading, teamed with a matching shade

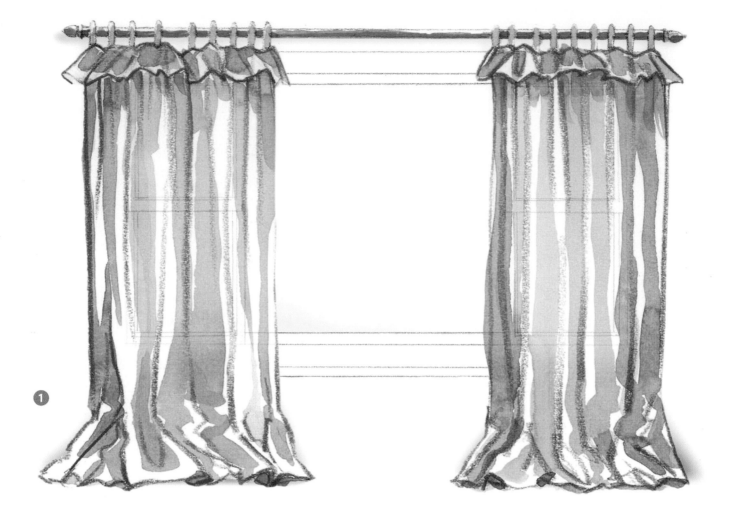

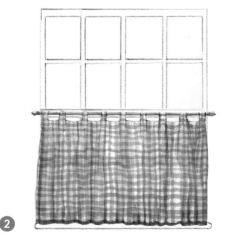

1 Puddled sheers with a curtain-ring heading

2 Tab-topped café curtain with a braided hem

3 Sill-length curtain with a central bowed tieback

4 Floor-length draperies with a gathered curtain-ring
   heading and roller shade

5 Double-tracked, tied-back draperies, the inner curtain in
   a sheer and the outer curtain in a heavy weave

③

④

⑤

1

2

1 Sill-length sheer with studded zigzag heading

2 Floor-length draperies with contrasting edging, fabric tiebacks, and scalloped cornice box

3 Denim-trimmed curtains with a leather rope-loop heading

4 Double-tracked draperies: the outer curtain in silk with a scalloped curtain-ring heading and the inner curtain in a light sheer

5 "Bishop's sleeve" curtain over a sheer

6 Multi-paneled Italian-strung curtains

3

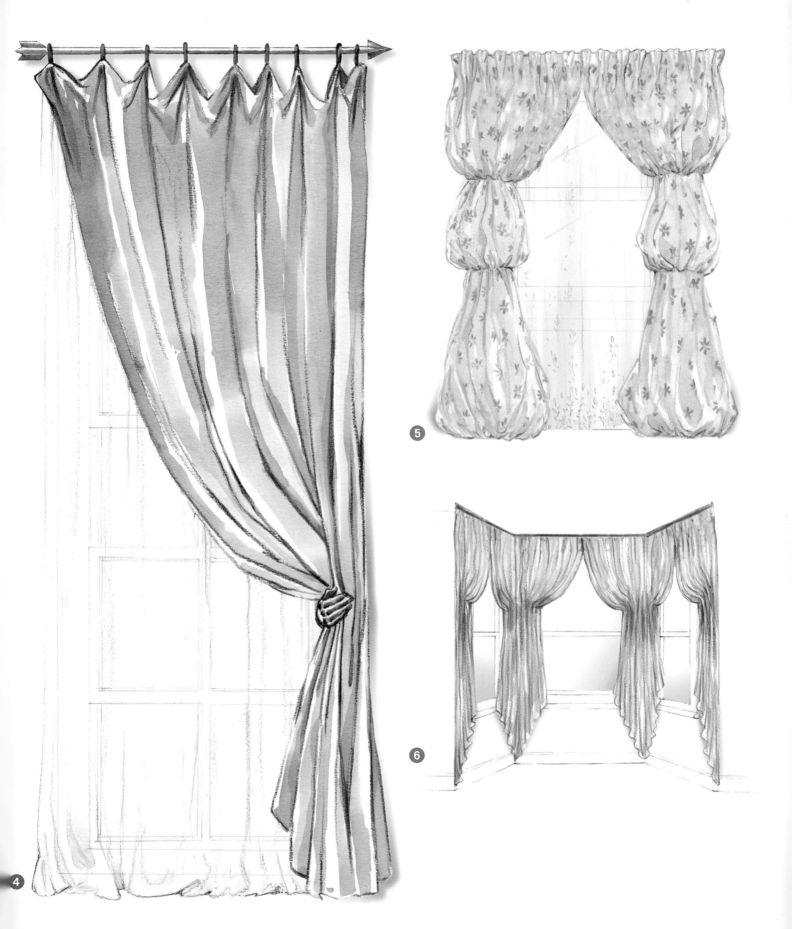

Swags and Scarves

A swag is a length of fabric draped across the top of the window to form a crescent shape; jabots are separate side pieces or "tails" that hang down to either side. Both elements are usually fixed to a board. A scarf is essentially a simpler and less formal way of achieving a swag-and-jabot treatment: it consists of a single length of fabric arranged over a pole or through a scarf holder.

A single scarf draped over a wrought-iron pole provides a means of introducing pattern in an otherwise monochromatic scheme.

Formal, traditional swag-and-jabot treatments rely on symmetry and neat pleating. The way the fabric hangs is critical, and heavier material will give a better result. The width of the window will determine the depth and number of swags. As a general rule, a swag should not extend more than 40 inches across and should be between 12 and 20 inches deep. Multiple swags should generally overlap slightly.

The jabot, which forms the vertical element of the treatment, can be styled to form a cascade or to make fluted or piped tubes. Jabots should be long enough to visually balance the swag or swags and may even extend down to the floor. They should always be lined because the underside will be revealed; a contrasting lining can be very effective.

Scarves are far less tailored than traditional swags and jabots. Instead of being fixed in place, they are arranged over decorative brackets or wrapped over poles. Lightweight or sheer fabrics are more suitable for this treatment than heavier fabrics because they are easier to drape and do not require lining. You may need to experiment with lengths of fabric to obtain the effect you wish to achieve.

Swags and scarves have much in common with valances. As a means of decorating the top of the window, they add a certain theatrical flourish. They can also be combined with other treatments, such as draperies, shades, or blinds, or featured on their own. Trimming in the form of fringing or tasseled cords can add to the decorative effect.

Scarves and swags can be used to decorate a wide variety of window types, either alone or in combination with other treatments. Where windows extend from floor to ceiling, the curved shapes of scarves and swags soften the lines and can help to make the windows seem wider than they actually are. Scarves and swags are equally effective where windows have a horizontal emphasis, or where there are multiple window units side by side.

2

1

1 Elegantly tailored single swags and jabots for a decorative flourish

2 Simple muslin scarves softening the lines of slatted shutters

3 A single coordinated scarf draped over a pole

4 A series of windows dressed with multiple scarves loosely wound around a pole

5 Period-style triple swag-and-jabot treatment, embellished with gold fringe

The French Empire style was flamboyant and conspicuously luxurious, both in the quantity of fabric required to create the flowing draperies and in the richness of material and trimmings. The style, which was set by Parisian upholsterers during the Napoleonic era, was hugely popular around the world. Many window treatments consisted of lightweight (often muslin) curtains topped with heavier draperies in a contrasting color, generally in the form of swags or scarves. The arrangement of the draperies was inspired by the flowing lines of antique Grecian dress, which also influenced women's fashions of the time. It was during this period that poles became both more visible and more decorative. Their designs were often vaguely militaristic, as befitting an imperial look.

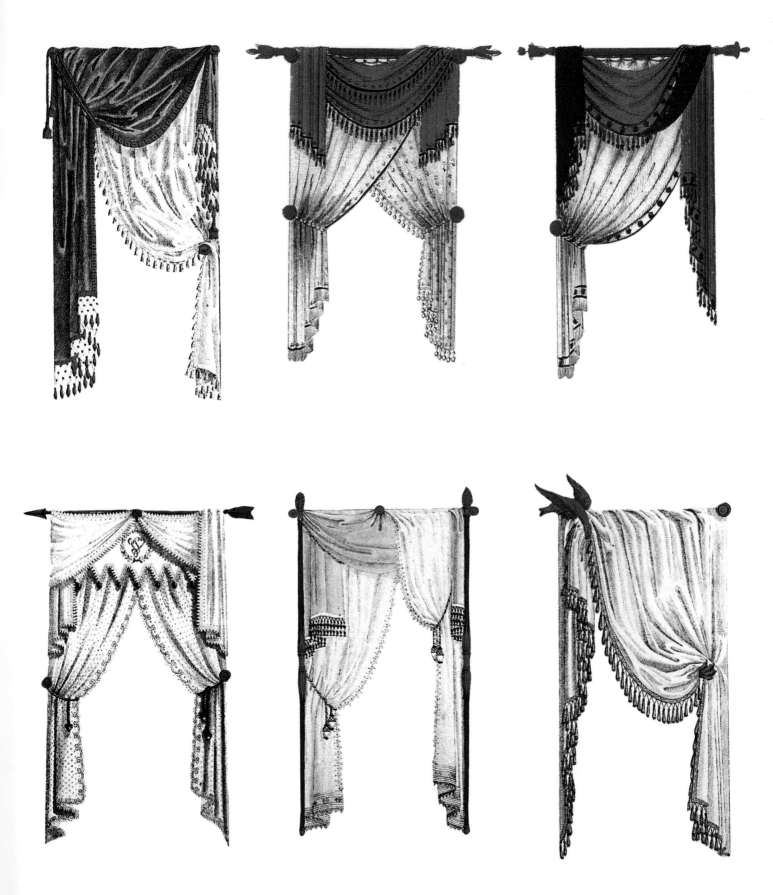

1–3 These elegant neoclassical designs for window draperies by the English furniture maker Thomas Sheraton are taken from his influential pattern book *The Cabinet-Maker, Upholsterer and General Artist's Encyclopedia*, 1804.

4 An opulent 1890s bedroom design by Georges Remon. It shows a retrospection to the earlier French Empire style as well as contemporary flowing silhouettes.

5–7 Geometric modernist designs by E. Thorne and H. Frohne, from *Decorative Draperies and Upholstery*, 1937. All additional ornament has been removed, to be replaced by a clean-lined functionalism.

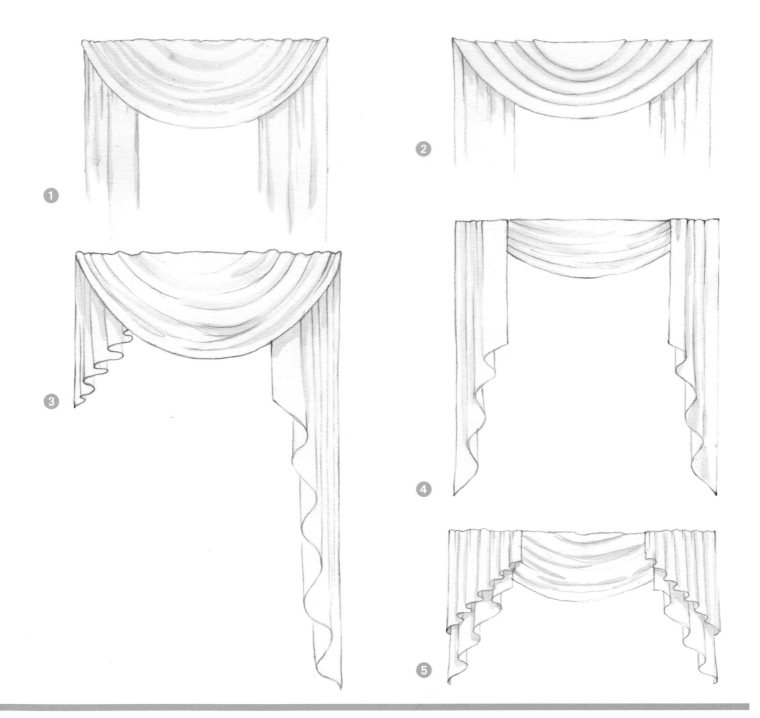

1   Single gathered swag

2   Pleated swag

3   Single swag with asymmetrical cascade jabots

4   Single swag with cascade jabots

5   With two-tiered cascade jabots

6   With gathered jabot

7   With knots

8   With rosettes

9   With double pipe jabots

10 With pleated jabots

11 Stretched over a shaped cornice

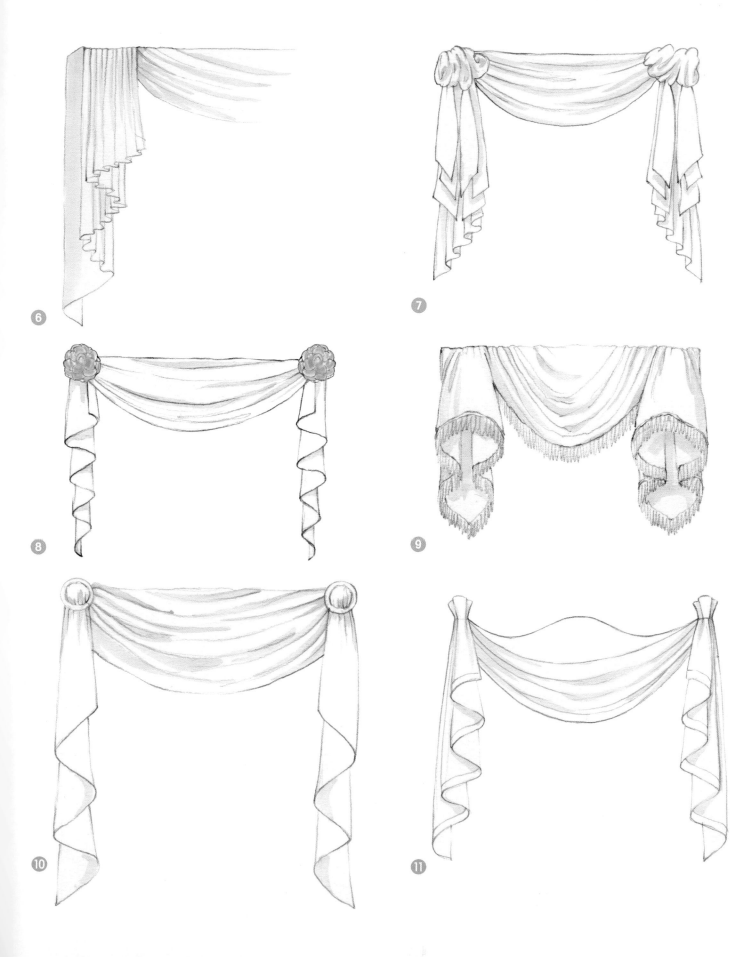

1

2

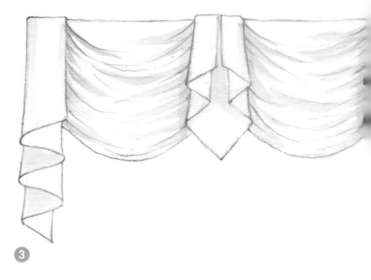

3

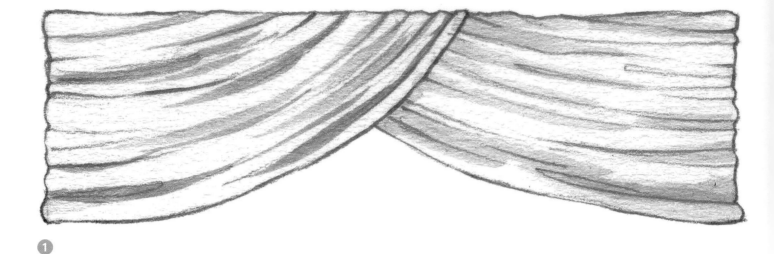

4

1 Turban swag

2 Asymmetrical swag with cascades

3 Multiple swag with pleated cascades

4 Double swag with cascades

5 Crown swag with cascades and central pipe jabot

6 Double swag with raised center

7 Waterfall swag

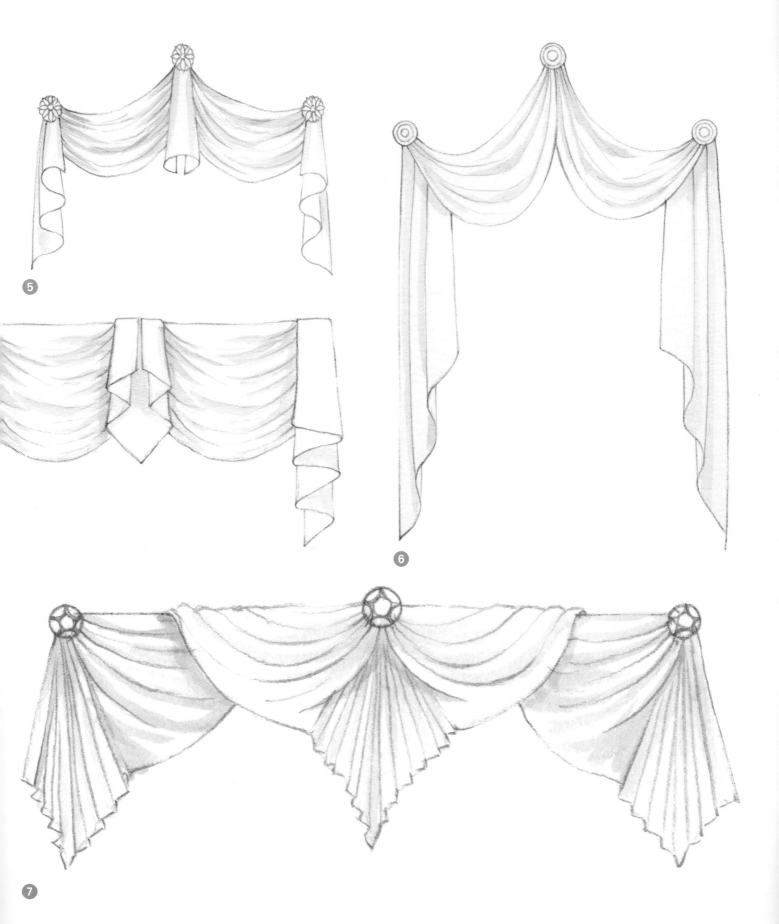

5

6

7

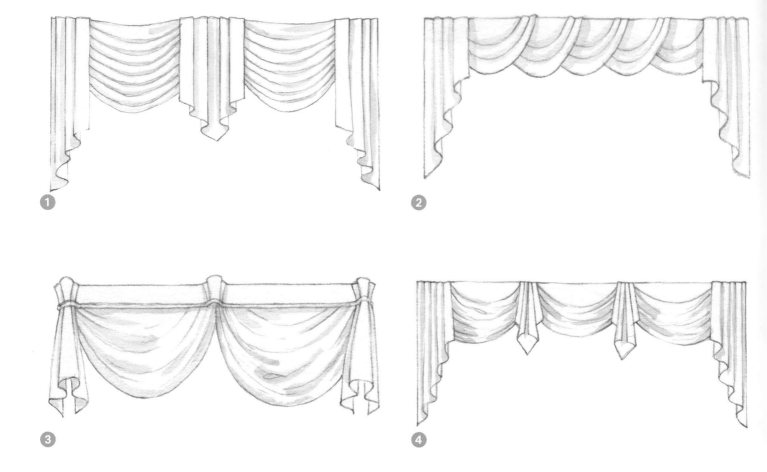

1 Double Empire-style swag

2 Multiple overlapping swag

3 Double swag with pleated jabots and braid

4 Triple swag with pleated pipe and cascade jabots

5 Double tail-free swag with bows

6 Triple swag

⑤

⑥

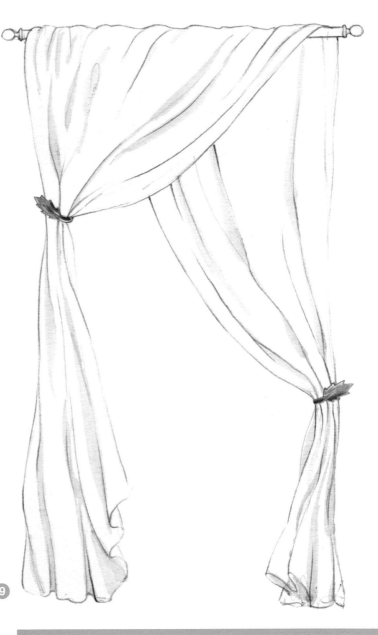

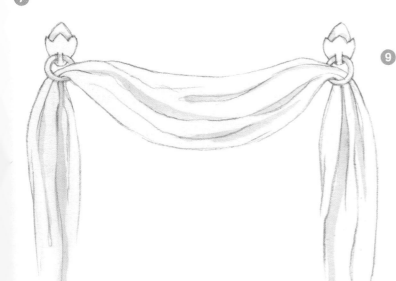

1 Asymmetrical draped pole

2 Billowing wrapped pole

3 Empire-style scarf

4 Double scarf with raised center

5 Triple scarf

6 Scarf with rosettes

7 Double crisscrossed scarf

8 Simple scarf through brackets

9 Crisscross-draped pole

Swags and Scarves

1 Multiple swags and cascade jabots with contrasting lining

2 Single gathered swag and jabots with gold trim

3 Silk scarf with rosette ties

4 Crisscross-draped pole in gold damask and pink silk

5 Casual knotted-and-looped scarf treatment in pale-pink voile

②

③

④

⑤

Swags and Scarves

1 Asymmetrical scarf with a tasseled Roman shade

2 Dramatic trimmed scarf treatment over puddled draperies

3 Asymmetrical scarf with contrasting lining and rosettes

4 Wrapped pole and floor-length silk curtains

5 Loose striped scarf with matching draperies

6 Double scarf with ample puddled draperies

7 Asymmetrical scarf over a wooden pole

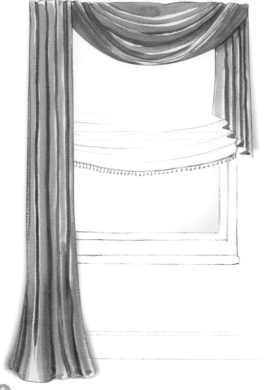

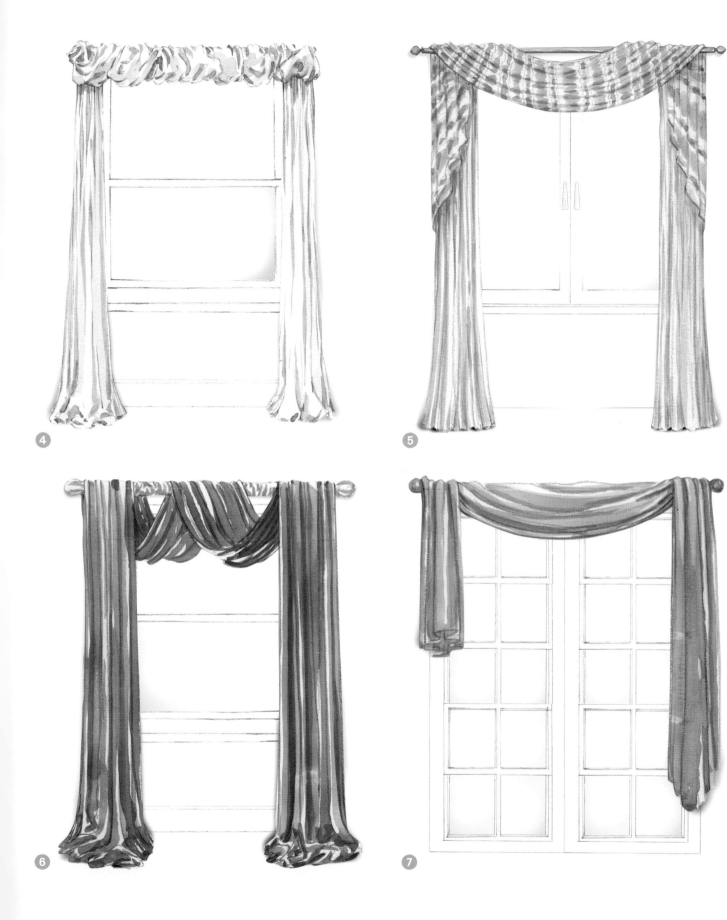

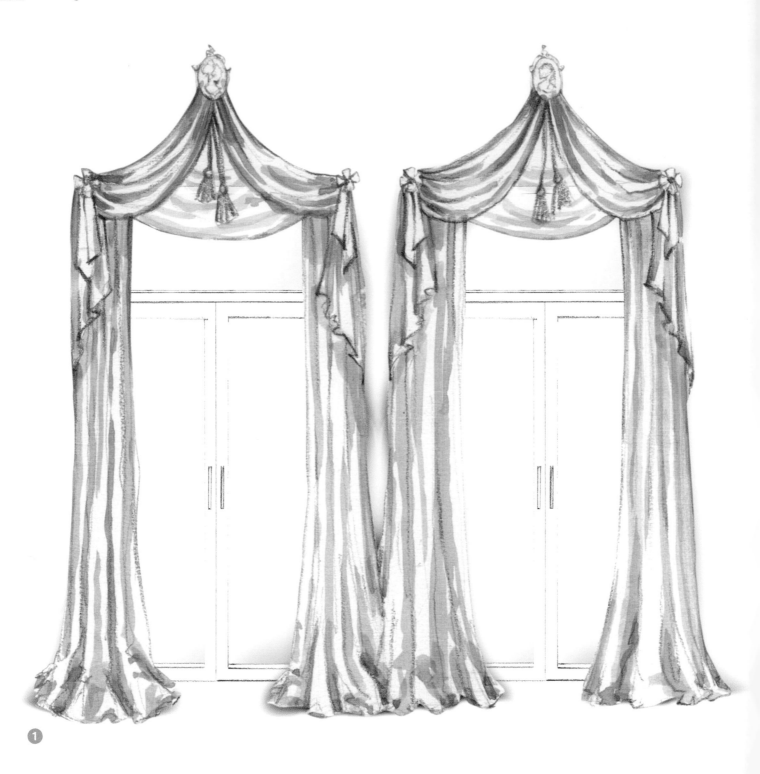

1

1 Elegantly trimmed crown swags with puddled draperies for a pair of French doors

2 Fringed triple scarf with cascade tails over tasseled tiebacks

3 Single scarf with rosettes and fringe over puddled draperies

4 Triple swag and jabots with embroidered draperies, framing a window seat

5 Double silk swag with a braid trim

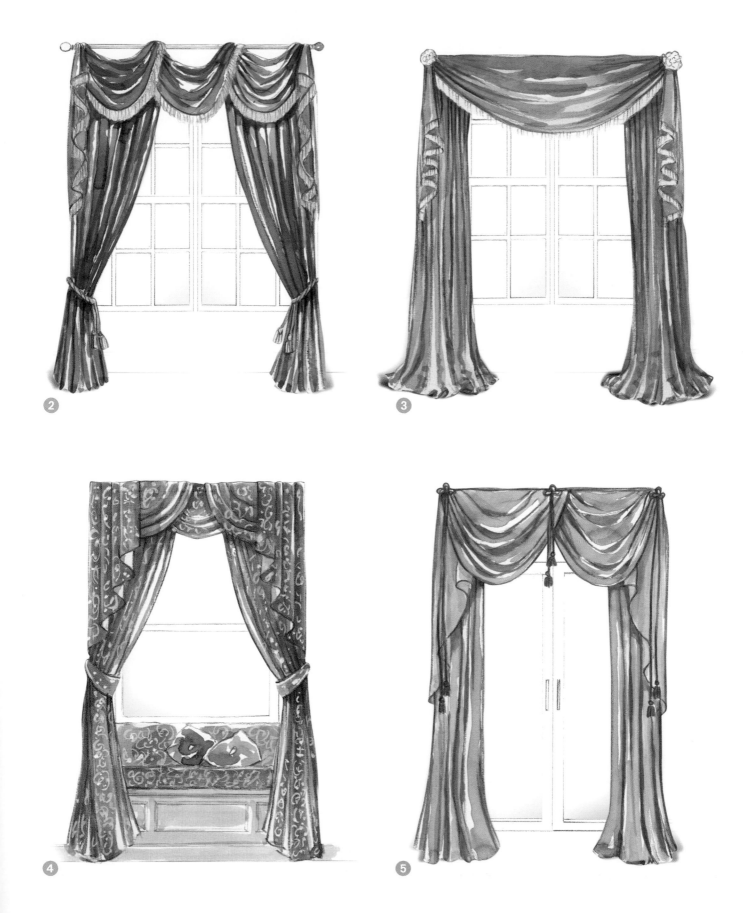

Fabrics

Window treatments provide the opportunity to showcase fabric. Whether fabric is displayed flat as a roller shade, hung in soft folds, or crisply pleated, its color, texture, and pattern will command attention. Fabric designated for furnishings comes in a huge range of weaves and designs. In addition, more unusual types of material, even dress fabrics, often make successful treatments.

Fabric's drape introduces a sense of movement that window treatments made of solid materials, such as shutters and blinds, lack. This single curtain with a deep foldover heading is held back low to form soft curved folds. The two contrasting geometric patterns accentuate the flowing lines of the treatment.

A fabric's weight governs how it can be used. Heavy materials suit the more structured type of heading: the weight allows curtains to hang in smooth, regular folds. Lighter materials are more informal and work better with shirred or gathered headings, or simple tie or tab tops.

Another important consideration is care. Fabrics such as silk, satin, and velvet require dry cleaning; some types of cotton may shrink if washed. Follow manufacturer's guidelines, and test-clean a swatch beforehand to judge the effect on weave and colorfastness.

Fabric is an instant way of adding color and pattern to your decorative scheme. Large-scale motifs are best displayed flat, while patterns that trail or branch suit applications where the material is gathered or folded. Geometric designs are always popular and suit both modern and traditional rooms. Such patterns, including checks, stripes, and dots, work well both in folds and as flat panels.

Texture is often underrated as a decorative element. Fabrics with obvious textures, such as velvet, brocade, and damask, have a tactility that lends a sense of warmth and luxury. Sheers and open weaves have an airy, breezy feeling.

Lining will improve the drape of most fabrics, while interlining will make curtains fully lightproof. Translucent fabrics, such as lace, muslin, and voile, do not require lining: the subtle way they diffuse light is all part of their appeal.

Dark, heavy fabrics, as well as those with an overt texture, have a warm, enclosing quality that makes a room feel more intimate and cozy. Lighter and semitranslucent fabrics are less formal in feeling and create an airy, breezy look. You may wish to adopt the traditional practice of changing the curtains on a seasonal basis, swapping heavy lined ones for light sheers or simpler styles in the summer months.

1 Heavy velvet curtains in navy blue for a note of elegance and formality

2 A light, summery cotton print teamed with a stagecoach shade

3 Crisp red stripes echoing the slatted louvers of wooden shutters

4 A simple blue check lining as a geometric foil for a willow pattern

5 Plain, light cotton for a fresh contemporary look

6 Lightweight unlined fabric tinting the light

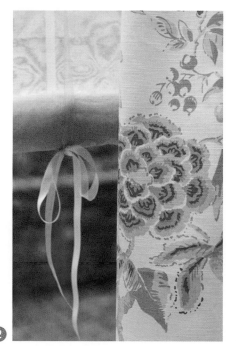

Fabric window treatments are often most successful when they coordinate with other soft furnishings. Matching pattern, color, and type of fabric is a tried-and-tested way of creating a harmonious scheme, but it can be a little relentless without at least some contrasting elements. Before you finalize a scheme, compare fabric swatches to determine how they work in combination. It is easy to partner solids with geometrics or floral prints when the same color is repeated.

4

1 Warm pink unifying a strong mix of florals and solids

2 A pretty floral pattern, repeated on curtains and bed coverings

3 Vivid orange-and-blue-striped silk for an injection of instant vitality

4 Green facing fabric lined in a contrasting pink stripe

5 Lustrous dupioni adds textural interest to a contemporary interior

5

97

Sheers and nets, which are designed to be used unlined, diffuse the light and create a soft ambiance. Ideal for light summery treatments or situations where you do not want to block light completely, they also provide an element of security and screen the interior from unwelcome views. There are a range of suitable fabrics, in both synthetic and natural fibers. Sheers suit simple headings and informal styles of treatment.

1 A semi-sheer voile with appliquéd seashells for a beachfront home

2 Double-tracked sheers for a supremely feminine look

3 Turquoise muslin curtains adding a jolt of color in a coordinated bedroom

4 Gray-striped sheers softening horizontal blinds

5 Nylon sheers with a denim stripe

Green is an inherently soothing shade. Particularly effective in natural, floral, or leaf designs, it also works well in crisp, geometric patterns. Complementary accents are red and pink. This family of patterns and colors is traditional without being unduly formal.

1 Cotton weaves (left to right): Art Nouveau-style rose pattern; Victorian-style poppy design; Arts and Crafts-style roses in burgundy

2 Fresh green gingham

3 Small red-and-green check

4 Textured cotton check

5 Plain cotton weave

6 Repeating vine print on cotton

7 Trailing leaf pattern on cotton

8 Pink-and-green plaid

9 Cotton children's print in the style of Kate Greenaway

10 Moiré plaid in blues and greens

11 Cotton rose print on an oatmeal background

12 Mint-green silk

13 Oriental-garden print

14 Dark-green cotton

15 Dusty-green velvet

16 Floral stripe in greens and pinks

17 Pistachio satin

6

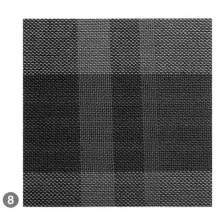

7

8

9

10

11

12

13

14

15

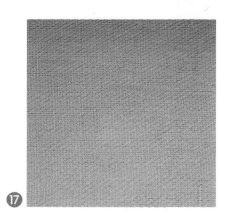

16

17

Neutrals, ranging from whites to biscuit or earth tones, are the mainstay of many furnishing schemes, classic or contemporary. When color is subdued, the emphasis falls on texture and material quality. Checks and stripes add graphic definition.

1 Clockwise from top left: chenille vine pattern; cocoa dupioni embroidered with metallic feathers; teardrop-roses weave in cream; Art Nouveau-style weave in oyster and terra-cotta

2 Equestrian design in tissue-pick Jacquard

3 Gold silk damask

4 Smocked linen

5 Silk weave with textured stripes

6 Checked silk

7 Metallic print on bronze silk

8 Gold-sheened synthetic mix

9 Pleated glazed silk

10 Butter-colored silk-polyester mix

11 Cotton Toile de Jouy

12 Corduroy velvet

13 Cotton oatmeal gingham

14 Cotton neutral stripe

15 Small check

16 Buttercup velvet

17 Textured check in brown and black

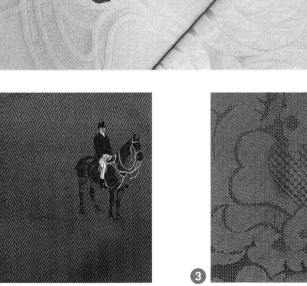

1

2

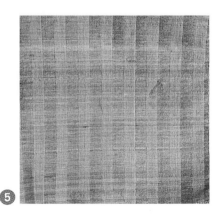

3

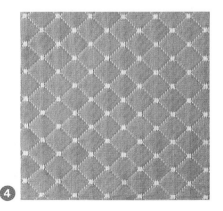

4

5

Unashamedly pretty, the palette that embraces the sweet pastel shades of pink, lilac, peach, and mauve is ideal for use in bedrooms. The feminine appeal of these gentle colors is enhanced by floral or embroidered patterns and touches of glitter. For a truly sumptuous and luxurious effect, choose silks or silk-type fabrics that have a reflective sheen and tactile quality.

1 Clockwise from left: paradise-garden print on sateen; large floral print on cotton damask base; Victorian screen-printed garden design; lavender repeating pattern on cotton

2 Purple-pink silk

3 Cream silk with dragonfly embroidery

4 Dusty-lilac silk

5 Trellis weave in lilac

6 Dusty-pink matte silk

7 Pink manmade weave

8 Pale Victorian print on silk

9 Purple-pink silk with silver sequins

10 Manmade heavy-textured weave in heather

11 Pale-pink gingham

12 Wild rose print on cotton

13 Dusty-pink polyester

14 Raspberry damask in mercerized cotton

15 Pale-pink satin

16 Peach herringbone-weave silk

17 Tapestry in pinks and blues

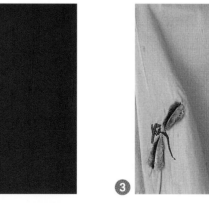

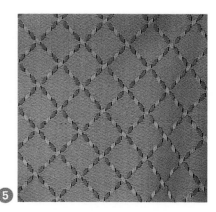

A fresh, contemporary mood is spelled out in the contrast of strong color. These designs, based on a pairing of blues and yellows, range from jaunty, maritime stripes to bold figurative prints, patterns that suit many different applications in the home. The crispness of the combination lends itself to cotton and linen fabrics and to tailored treatments and fabric shades.

1 Clockwise from left: embroidered pale-blue silk; washed denim with poppy embroidery; bright-blue floral print on white cotton

2 Yellow silk with teardrop sequins

3 Baby-blue silk

4 Dotted blue-check weave

5 Blue-and-gold woven stripe

6 Blue floral print on a lemon background

7 Lisere Jacquard weave in buttercup

8 Blue-and-yellow plaid

9 Deep-blue silk

10 Pale-blue gingham

11 Deep-blue linen

12 Lemon damask

13 Yellow gingham

14 Brocade with a gold beetle design

15 Palm-embroidered indigo denim

16 Jacquard-woven denim

17 Pale-blue linen

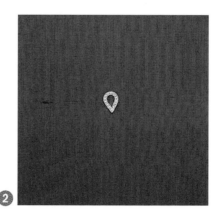

6

7

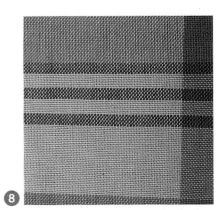

8

9

10

11

12

13

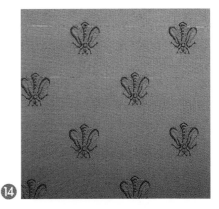

14

15

16

17

Rich colors at the warm end of the
spectrum, such as reds, purples, and golds,
are inherently opulent. Both traditional
patterns and textural fabrics accentuate the
effect—choose velvet, damask, chenille,
and satin if you are after a distinguished
period look.

1 Clockwise from left:
   red-and-gold
   brocade; floral
   brocade on a
   cranberry ground;
   burgundy damask

2 Scarlet check

3 Foliage print
   in burgundy

4 Lipstick-red satin

5 Burgundy cotton
   check

6 Coral fern print

7 Red-and-purple
   plaid

8 Flame-colored silk

9 Aztec-style tapestry

10 Red-and-gold silk
   taffeta plaid

11 Red damask

12 Kilim-style chenille

13 Oriental-garden
   print on cotton

14 Children's animal
   print on cotton

15 Embroidered
   scarlet silk

16 Claret cotton with
   gold dots

17 Sailing-boat pattern
   in Jacquard weave

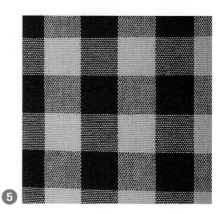

6

7

8

9

10

11

12

13

14

15

16

17

Sheers or semitranslucent fabrics come in a range of transparencies, depending on weave and fiber type. The most decorative is lace, which looks particularly effective hung in flat panels directly against a window. Other patterns include dotted weaves, embroidered designs, and floral motifs. Colored sheers add a touch of theatricality. All sheers are delicate and lightweight, making them ideal for draping or simple, unstructured treatments.

1 Silk sheer with an embroidered floral design

2 Bluebell-pattern lace

3 Floral lace

4 Bold rose-pattern lace

5 Fern-pattern lace

6 Traditional rose-pattern lace

7 Floral lace

8 Lace with daisy detail

9 Fleur-de-lis muslin

10 Dotted lace

11 Star-pattern lace

12 Wide-weave oatmeal floral lace

13 White cotton broderie anglaise

14 Oatmeal foliage-pattern lace

15 Striped semi-sheer

16 Wide-striped voile

17 White voile

18 Floral-pattern crinkle voile

19 Classical-print voile

20 Polyester-cotton with denim stripe

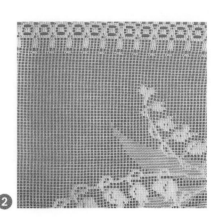

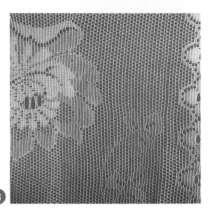

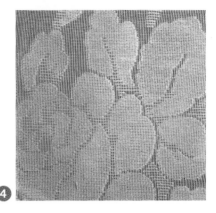

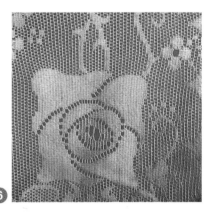

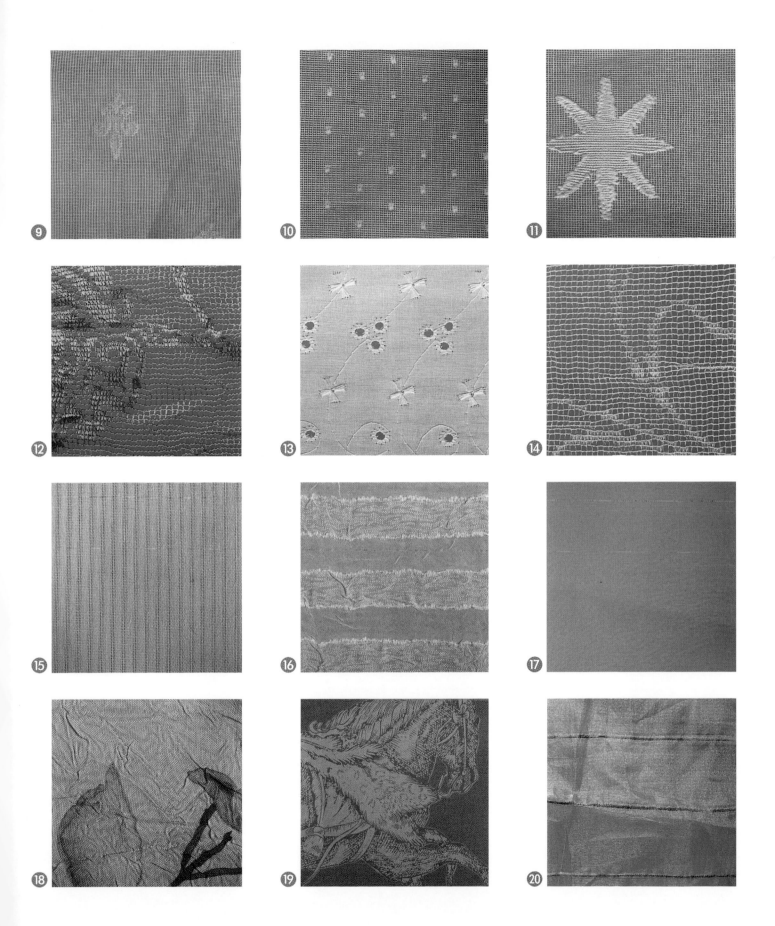

Valances

Valances are a means of dressing, and adding interest to, the top of the window. In purely practical terms, they provide a way of hiding hardware, tracks, and cords that may not be designed for display. A valance can also be used to correct proportions. Depending on the depth of the valance and where it is positioned, it can visually shorten, lengthen, widen, or streamline a window.

Valances are always made of fabric and share the same heading options and means of suspension as curtains. Like curtains, valance headings may be shirred along a rod, gathered into soft folds, pleated, or tabbed. Other styles include the balloon valance, which is gathered into billows like a festoon shade, and the pennant valance, with separate panels of fabric draped over the length of a rod. Shaped hems and trimming provide additional interest.

As a basic rule of thumb, valances should not extend more than a quarter of the way down the window, while the tails of a shaped valance should extend no further than a third. Valances work well with a wide range of window treatments and may even be used on their own to trim the window top.

Although they are most often teamed with curtains, valances lend a softening element to harder treatments such as blinds and shutters as well as combining easily with fabric shades. You can also partner a shallow upholstered cornice with a valance attached to its lower edge.

One tried-and-tested formula for valances designed to accompany curtains is to match both the heading style and the type of fabric, so the overall effect is unified. But striking contrasts of heading style and fabric extend the decorative possibilities further. Valances can also be improvised out of unusual materials or fabrics that are not traditionally used for furnishings.

A valance gathered in the center and teamed with matching curtains frames a cozy windowseat.

1

Valances serve to disguise hardware while providing a well-considered, finished look. Coordinating valances with curtains is a popular option; but bold contrasts of color, pattern, and fabric can also be very effective.

1 Striped gathered valance and matching curtains

2 Formal valances coordinate with a draped bed

3 A scalloped valance in toile de Jouy

4 Soft eyelet lace valance

5 Contrasting cotton valance

2

3

4

5

Always a versatile treatment, a valance can be used as a feature on its own to frame a window and soften its lines or to make more tailored window coverings, such as blinds and shutters, appear less severe and uncompromising. Decorative valances, such as cloud or balloon types, which closely resemble festoon shades, add a theatrical, feminine flourish to the window top.

1 A box-pleated valance in narrow stripes as a tailored accompaniment to blinds

2 Sheer valances softening the hard lines of Venetian blinds

3 A pretty scalloped lace valance delicately framing a view

4 A cloud valance in contrasting prints

The 19th century was the heyday of the valance, when it was used to its most dramatic effect. Rather than being seen as a decorative accessory to the window treatment, it was conceived as a central and defining part of the design scheme.

1–4 By the end of the 18th century, box cornices had given way to billowing draped valances, often incorporating rosettes, tassels, and other forms of trimming. For these French Empire-style draperies, the entire treatment was conceived as a whole.

5–6 British examples of early 19th-century draperies reveal the neoclassical fascination with the motifs of ancient Egypt and other antique civilizations.

7–11 These 1826 designs combine solid carved cornices with elaborately draped and trimmed valances.

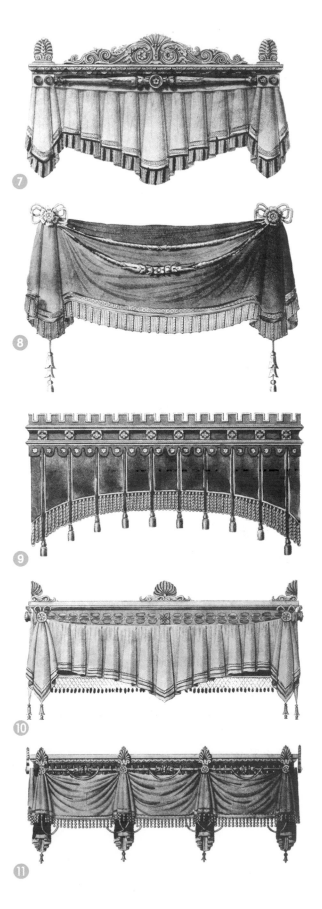

5

6

7

8

9

10

11

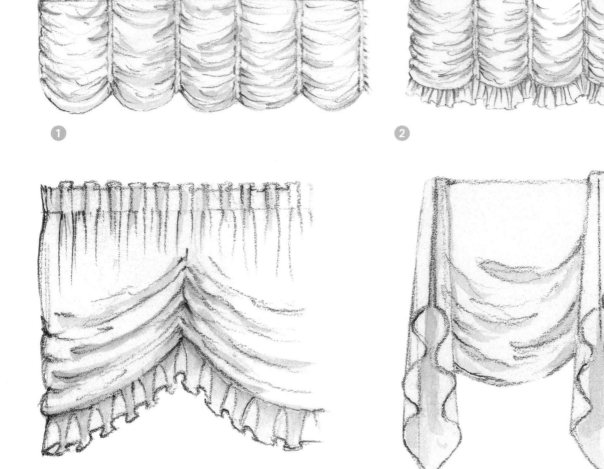

① ②

③ ④

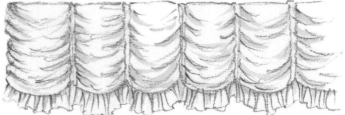

⑤

⑥

1	Austrian	
2	Austrian with ruffle	
3	Pencil pleat with Austrian gathers and ruffle	
4	Austrian with jabots	
5	Balloon valance	
6	Balloon with piping	
7	Cloud with rod pocket	
8	Cloud with ruffle on rod pocket	
9	Cloud with ruffle on double rods	
10	Puff	
11	Balloon valance with tails	

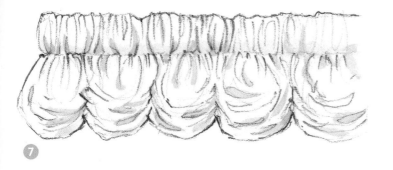

7

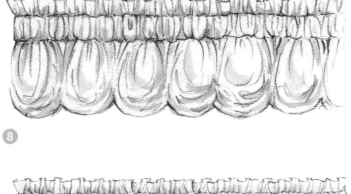

8

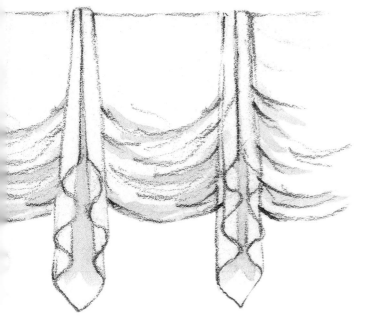

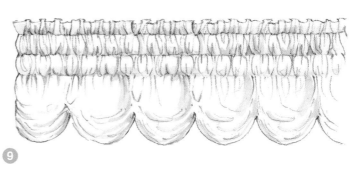

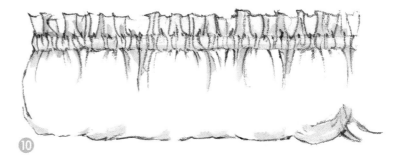

9

10

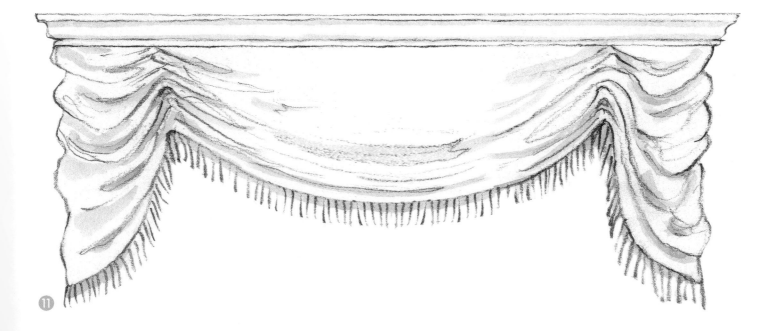

11

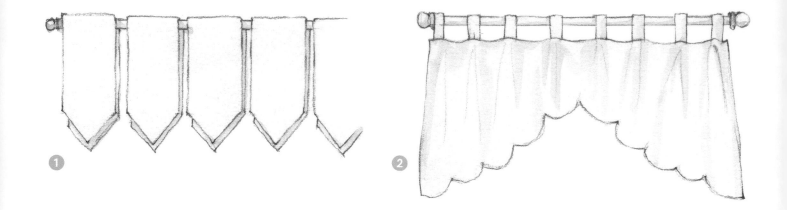

1 Banner

2 Scalloped

3 Crenellated

4 Tabbed

5 Bow tie

6 Ribbon and eyelet

7 Inverted box pleat with tabs

8 Pinch pleat with arch

9 Teardrop

10 Tented

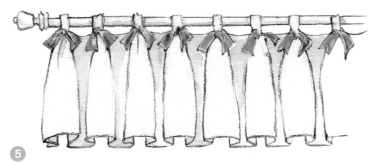

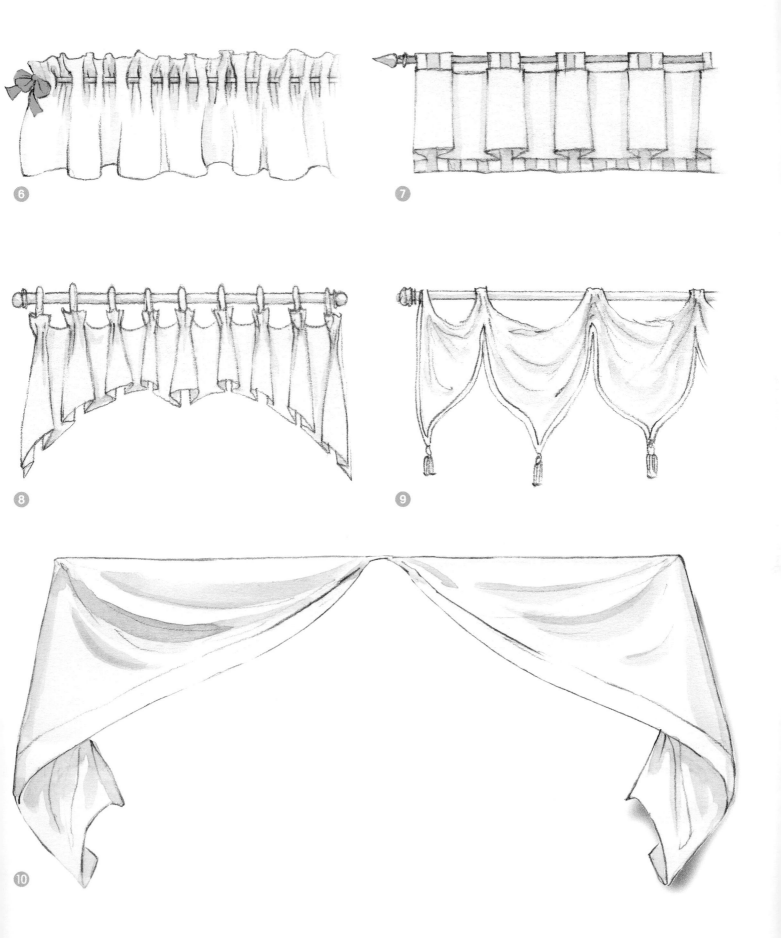

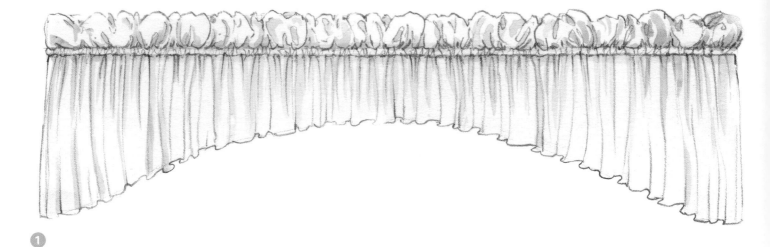

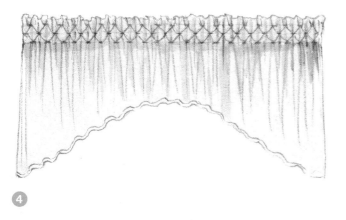

1. Gathered with rod pocket and puff

2. Gathered with rod pocket and ruffle

3. Petticoat

4. Smocked and gathered arch

5. Gathered with braiding and tassels

6. Rod pockets with arched top

7. Gathered with arched top

8. Double rod pocket with decorative rods

9. Triple rod pocket

10. Double rod pocket with ruffle

11. Gathered with multiple rod pockets

12. Double-arched rod pocket with ruffle

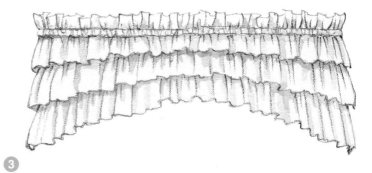

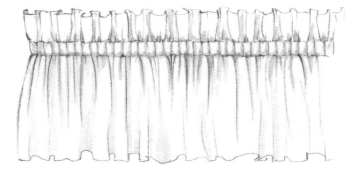

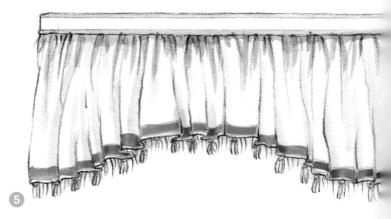

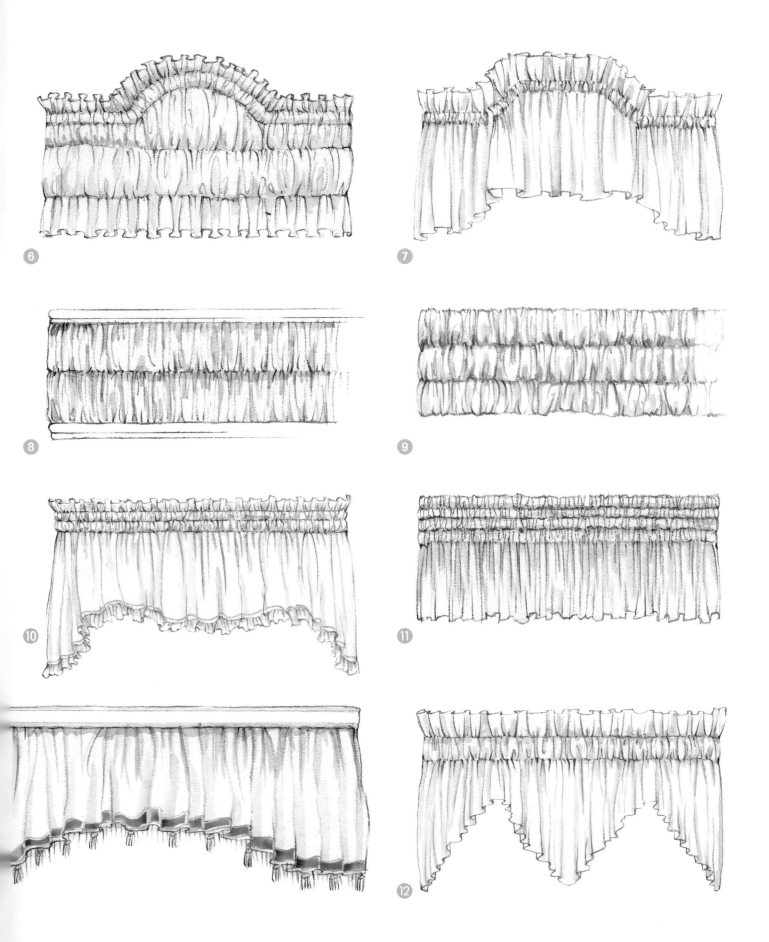

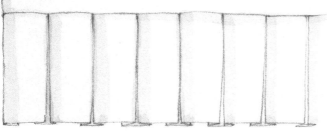

1   Stepped inverted box pleat

2   Inverted box pleat

3   Pennant

4   Pinch pleat

5   Pinch pleat with gathered scallop

6   Double pinch pleat

7   Double pinch with scallop

8   Pinch pleat with arch

9   Bell pleat

10   Pencil pleat with ruffle

11   Triple cartridge pleat

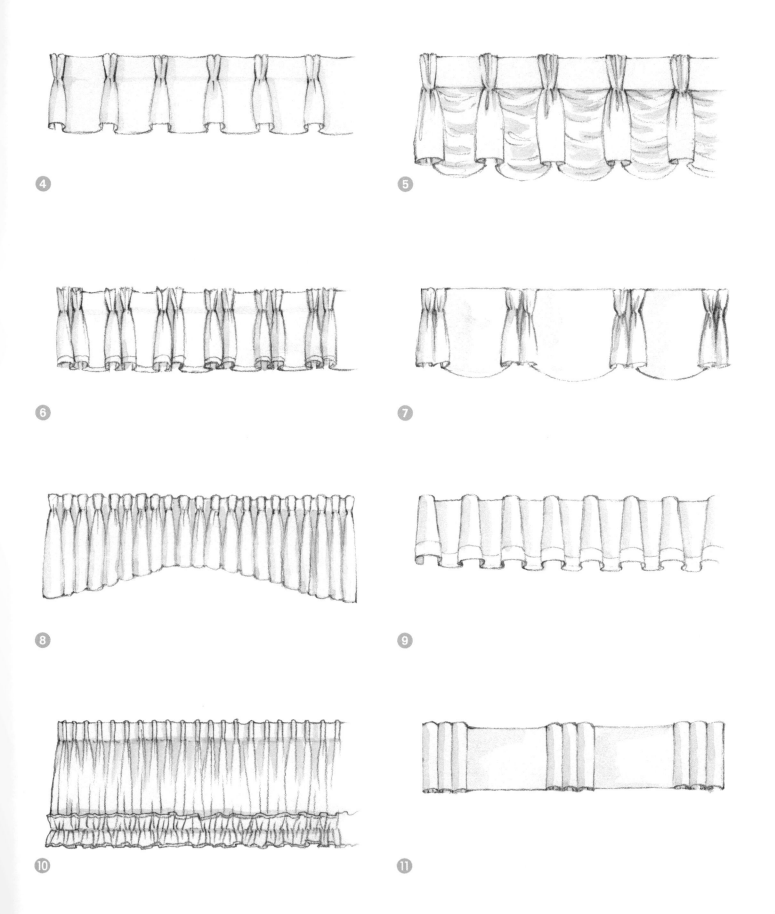

Valances

1 Sheer scarf valance with tassel trim

2 Long pennant valance dressing a tall,
   thin window

3 Crenellated valance and a roller shade

4 Banner valance and a Roman shade with
   contrasting trim

5 Gathered valance with floor-length tiebacks
   and a roller shade

6 Balloon valance with puddled draperies
   in silk

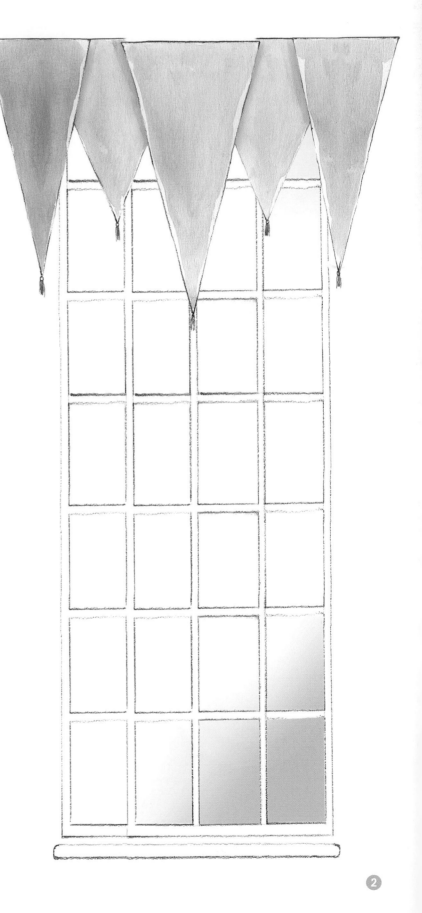

1

2

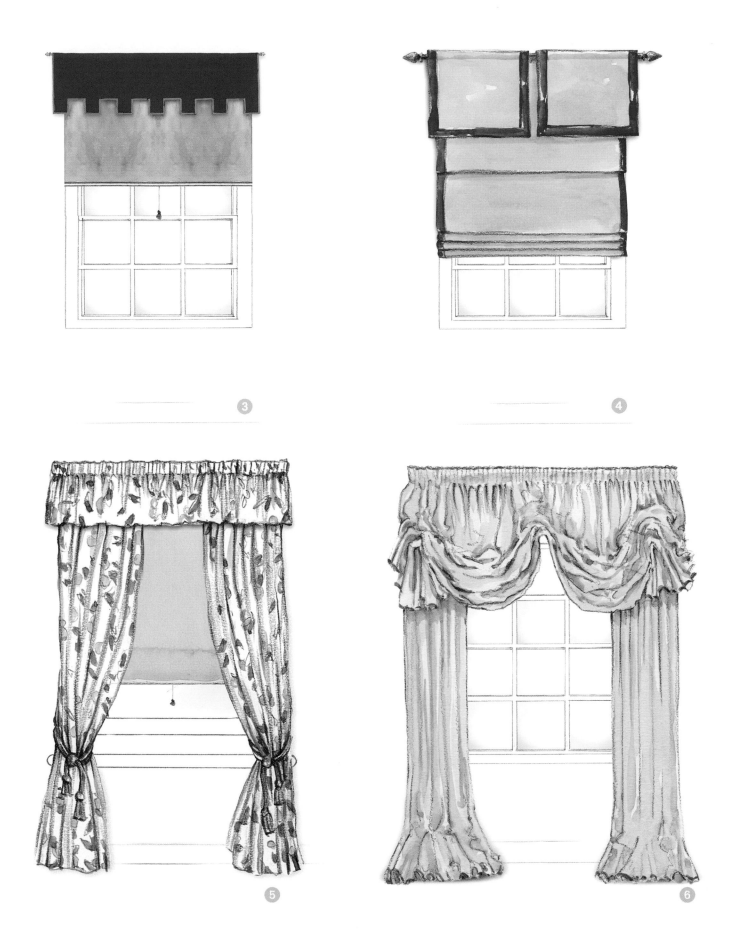

3

4

5

6

1

1 Gathered valance hung from pegs with floor-length curtains

2 Stepped inverted box pleat with gold braid

3 Tailed valance and a sheer café curtain

4 Balloon valance teamed with a plastic miniblind

5 Trimmed Austrian valance with floor-length draperies

6 Gathered valance and pinned-back draperies in a heavy damask

2

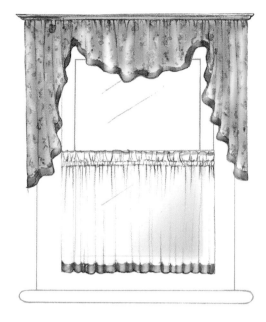

3

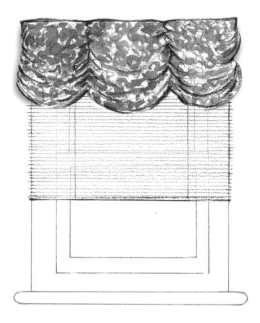

4

5

6

Cornices and Lambrequins

Like valances, cornices and lambrequins dress the top of the window, but—while valances are made of fabric—these treatments tend to be constructed from stiffer materials such as wood or board. Traditional or contemporary, cornices and lambrequins can be adapted to any style of interior and to complement a wide variety of window treatments, from curtains to blinds and shutters.

A suitably clean-lined treatment for a contemporary room, this simple white box cornice features a check fabric-panel insert, adding a graphic contrast to the plain blue shade.

Cornices and lambrequins serve the same practical role as valances, providing a convenient way of concealing less decorative types of hardware and helping to correct any deficiencies in window shape or proportion. For example, you can make a short window appear longer by installing a cornice so that it covers the portion of wall above the window frame. Conversely, you can shorten the apparent length of a long window by installing a cornice so it covers the upper portion of the window. Similarly, cornices can also be a unifying element where windows differ in shape or size.

The most common type of cornice is the box cornice, which is generally made of wood and may be trimmed with molding or upholstered and accessorized. Box cornices lend architectural distinction to window treatments. If the cornice is to remain a permanent feature, keep it relatively plain and match the detailing to moldings elsewhere in the room. The other type of cornice is shaped, in which the front is replaced with stiffened fabric cut in a decorative shape.

Lambrequins are more extravagant versions of cornices, in which the sides extend at least two thirds of the way down the window. These are often decoratively shaped and upholstered to add richness to the window treatment.

When choosing a cornice or lambrequin, keep in mind the decorative style of the room. A dramatic cornice could be the essential finishing touch to a rich design scheme, but could also overwhelm more simple details.

1 A scallop-edged cornice covered in blue check fabric for added interest to plain sill-length curtains

2 Echoing the color of the walls, a vivid yellow-painted wooden cornice embellished with a fun fish motif

3 A unified effect created by matching cornices to draperies

4 A cream-painted wooden cornice setting off a blue and green Roman shade

Cornices make elegant finishing touches to window treatments. Although they are essentially solid, made of stiff materials such as wood and board, their appearance may be softened with fabric. When a cornice is upholstered, it is important to choose a fabric that looks good when displayed flat. Geometric or repeat patterns work better in this way than branching designs. Painted wooden cornices often look best when the color matches other woodwork or the walls.

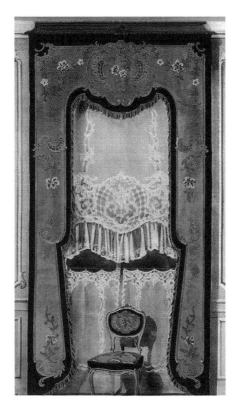

These late 19th-century French designs for cornices and lambrequins date from a period when windows were elaborately decorated with many layers of fabric. The cornice or lambrequin provided a vehicle for decorative shaping and embellishment, framing the draperies and shades suspended behind it. Such richness and complexity are typical of the cluttered look in interior decoration. This first came into fashion in 1850s Paris and then spread around the world, reaching its height of popularity in the late 1880s and early 1890s. As these designs reveal, the cornice or lambrequin was typically upholstered and trimmed to match the main outer draperies. Sheers, known as "glass" curtains and usually made of lace, were hung on rods to complete the look.

The cornice evolved as a useful means of concealing curtain hardware, which remained utilitarian in appearance until the beginning of the 19th century. Eighteenth-century examples of cornices, designed by cabinetmakers, show a conscious attempt to echo architectural detailing, with cornices displaying either classical moldings or Baroque-style flourishes. Later cornice styles were more closely tied to the style of the window treatment itself.

CROISÉE RENAISSANCE.

COUPES ET DÉTAILS DE LA CROISÉE _ Nº 1749.

1 An elegant 1890s French curtain design with a scalloped cornice, named "Croisée Renaissance"

2 Delicate, richly ornamented cornices by Thomas Sheraton, taken from *The Cabinet-Maker and Upholsterer's Drawing Book*, 1793

3 Rococo cornices by Thomas Chippendale, from his influential *The Gentleman and Cabinet-Maker's Director*, 1759

4 An early 20th-century window seat crowned by a gracefully shaped cornice and enclosed by floral draperies

5 An 1890s watercolor of a bedroom window framed by matching cornice and tiebacks

1 Scalloped fabric-covered cornice with gathered drapery and star details

2 Box cornice with shirred fabric panel and jabots

3 Fabric-covered shaped cornice with swags and jabots

4 Arched cornice with pinch pleats and a braid

5 Turban cornice

6 Hourglass-shaped cornice with fabric panel

7 Arched shirred cornice

8 Shirred box cornice with a top and bottom braid

9 Arched quilted cornice with tassels

10 Box cornice with shirred panels

11 Box cornice with shirred bottom panel

12 Fabric-covered box cornice with a contrasting braid

13 Box cornice with swags and jabots

14 Shaped cornice with ruffle

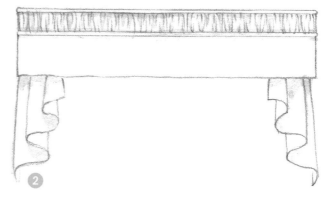

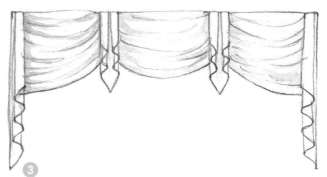

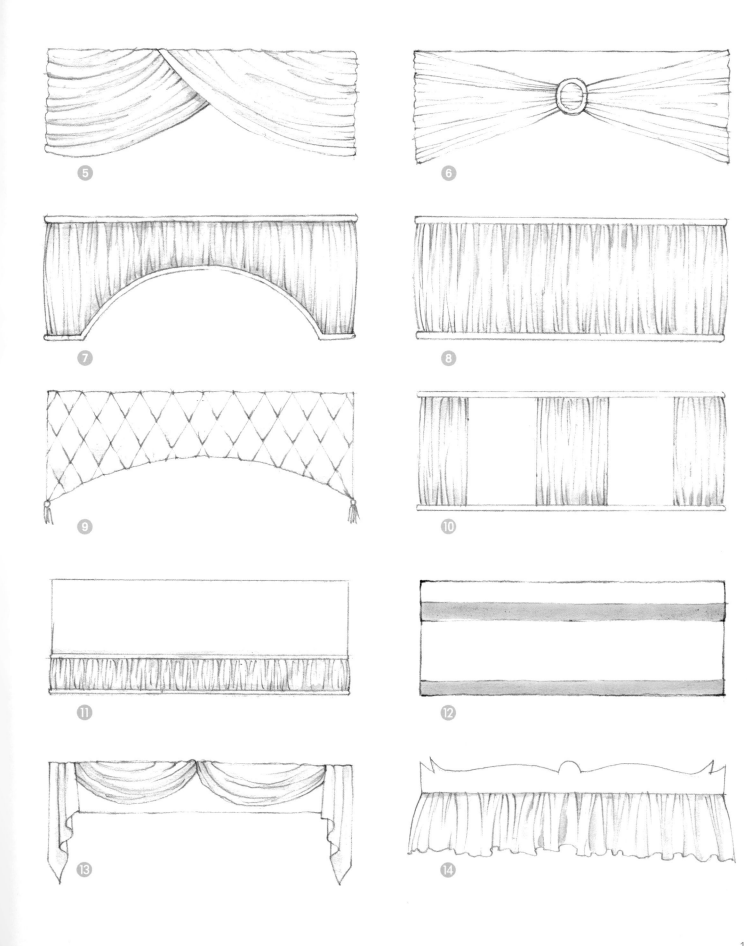

1 Scalloped cornice with shirred band

2 Box cornice covered with pleated fabric

3 Arched cornice with a contrasting braid

4 Box cornice with ruffle

5 Box cornice with fabric band

6 Fabric-covered pennant cornice

7 Scalloped cornice with pleated band

8 Scalloped cornice with a contrasting braid

9 Box cornice with horizontal pleats

10 Wooden box cornice with painted floral design

11 Beehive cornice

12 Traditionally shaped wooden cornice

13 Crenellated and painted wooden cornice

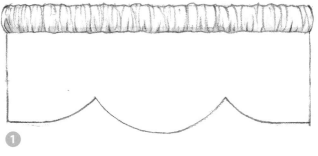

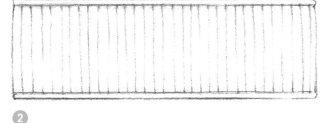

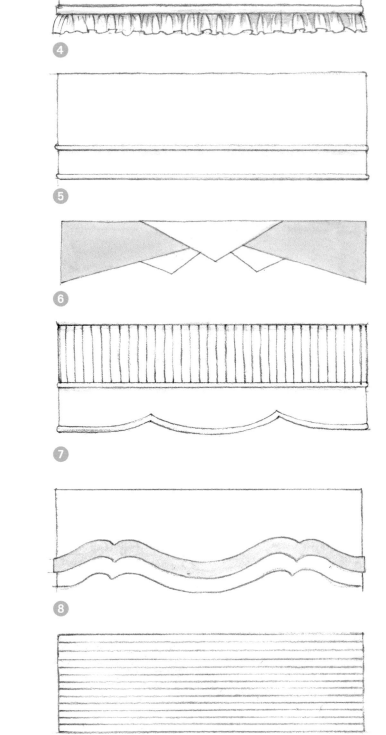

10

11

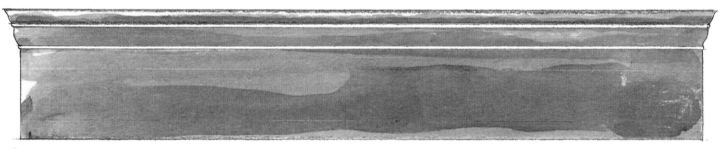

12

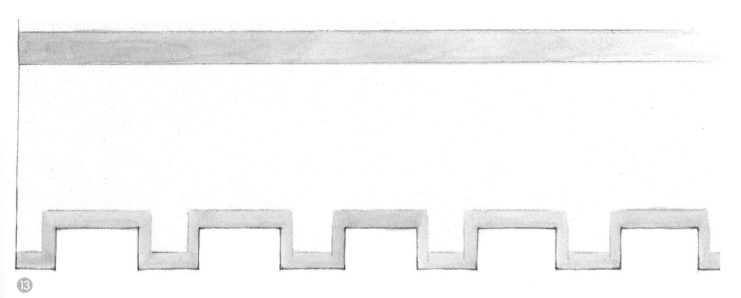

13

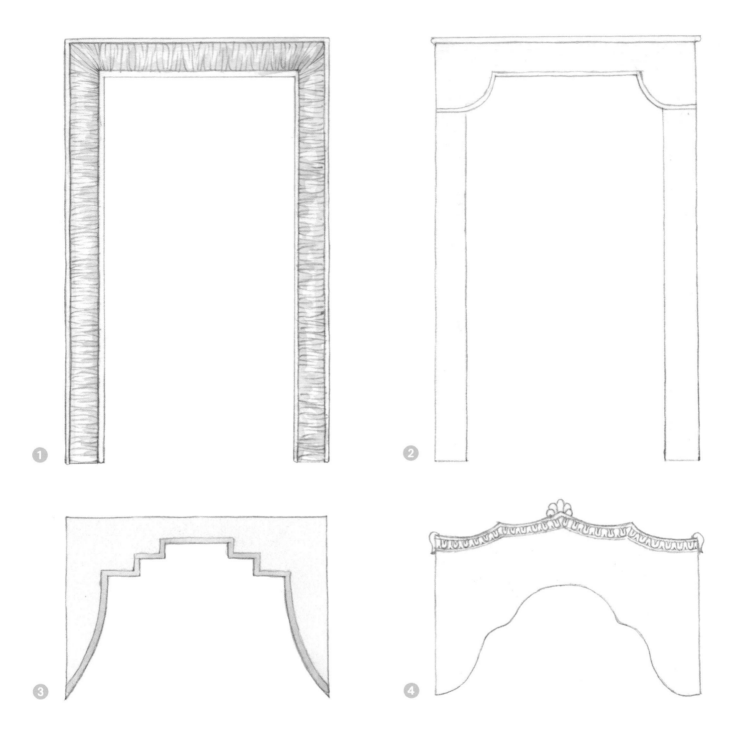

1 Shirred rectangular lambrequin

2 Shaped lambrequin with welt edge

3 Geometric painted lambrequin with contrasting edge

4 Shaped lambrequin with decorative plaster crown

5 Rectangular lambrequin covered in floral fabric

6 Geometric wooden lambrequin

7 Scalloped fabric-covered lambrequin

8 Plain wooden arched lambrequin

1 Antique gilt cornice with a box-pleat valance and puddled damask draperies

2 Cushioned box cornice with matching floor-length curtains

3 "Handkerchief-point" fabric-covered cornice and simple tiebacks

4 Scalloped cornice dressed with black trim and tassels, teamed with black-bordered floor-length draperies

5 Fabric-covered box-pleated cornice with matching check curtains

2

3

4

5

Cornices and Lambrequins

1 Fabric-covered box cornice and muslin curtains, with loop tiebacks in a matching print

2 Shaped fabric-covered cornice with tasseled tiebacks and scalloped roller shades, trimmed with tassels

3 Tapestry-covered cornice with a Roman shade

4 Oak traditional-style cornice with off-white folding shutters

5 Painted wooden cornice with puddled sheers

6 Shaped cornice trimmed with a braid, matching draperies, and sheer inner curtains

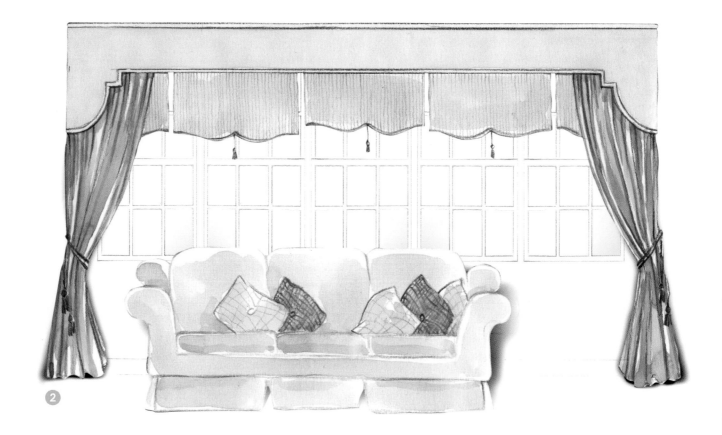

3

4

5

6

Shades

The fabric shade is a versatile and popular window treatment. It can be used on a wide variety of window types, including problem windows, and in combination with other forms of treatment. Because a fabric shade generally uses much less material than curtains, it is also very economical.

Strictly speaking, shades consist of single pieces of fabric that are raised or lowered over the window. The most common form is the roller shade, which is operated by a spring mechanism. More tailored is the Roman shade, which pulls up into deep pleats. Festoon shades, which have headings like curtains, are the most decorative variety, and draw up into soft, luxurious billows.

The fabric shade is a great problem solver. It allows you to make fine adjustments to both the amount of privacy and the degree of light a room receives because it can be lowered or raised to any level. While most shades operate from the top, bottom-mounted shades pull up from the sill. This enables you to block views and maintain privacy while allowing light in at the top. In areas where full-length curtains may not be advisable, such as kitchens and bathrooms, shades make a practical, no-nonsense solution.

However, it would be wrong to think of the shade as exclusively a functional treatment. Festoons are, of course, highly decorative, but even simpler shade styles lend themselves to trimming and embellishment. Shades also work extremely well with other types of window treatments. In combination with curtains, or even with blinds, they offer optimum flexibility.

These richly colored and opulent silk cloud shades have a delicately shirred heading.

1 Three separate roller shades made of sheer fabric as a unifying treatment for windows of different sizes

2 A shade made of rough burlap filtering the light

3 A strongly textural effect with a basket-woven straw shade

4 A shade in a cheerful nursery print combined with a soft fabric valance in a striped design

5 A scalloped-and-beaded edge for added decorative interest

Roller and roll-up shades are simple and economical. They are generally made of stiffened fabric, but they may also be made of vinyl, sheer fabric, or even woven cane, wood, or straw. A plain white roller shade is the most restrained type of window treatment around. The addition of some color and pattern will strike a livelier note. You can also purchase shades made of blackout material to exclude light completely. These shades should be hung so that they just cover the window frame. If the window is inset, a shade may be positioned to hang against the glass. Some types of roller shades incorporate a pull that lets you raise or lower the shade without handling the edge of the fabric. Wooden-, metal-, or bead-handled cords or pulls can add an extra decorative element.

The Roman shade is an elegant, classic treatment that works well both in period and contemporary interiors. Softer-looking than a roller shade but more tailored than a festoon, the Roman shade pulls up into deep horizontal folds and coordinates well with curtains. You need to exercise a degree of care over your choice of pattern. Large or overly busy designs detract somewhat from the clean lines: plain or textured material often looks better. Roman shades may be neatly trimmed with contrast binding or edging. They can also be lined if you are looking for a more substantial or light-filtering effect.

1 A Roman shade with a shaped edge to complement the pretty floral print

2 Beaded trimming accentuating the delicacy of a Roman shade made of sheer voile, combined with draperies

3 Roman shades in a sheer weave installed part of the way down the frame to expose decorative leaded lights

4 Neat cotton Roman shades trimmed with contrasting braid

5 A Roman shade in a botanical print with a scalloped edge held by a metal rod

1

More decorative types of shades include pleated versions and various forms of festoons. Festoons are supremely romantic and theatrical treatments. Depending on the fabric, the type of heading, and the way the fabric is gathered at the base of the shade, the effect can be soft and balloon-like or more billowy, as in a cloud shade. Suitable headings include gathered, pleated, or shirred. Lining improves the shape. Festoons hang fairly low down, which means they suit large and tall windows better than small ones. Some types are stationary. The effect of these shades is enhanced by decorative trimming with lace and ruffles.

1 A pleated fabric shade in accordion folds over the window

2 Stagecoach shade in a floral print, lined in contrasting fabric and secured by bows

3 A side-gathered shade creating a decorative flourish over a sheer roller

4 A sheer roll-up shade with bands of contrasting-textured fabrics

5 A pretty cascade shade as a finishing touch for a feminine bedroom

3

4

2

5

1 A design for an "Italian ruched" shade comes complete with instructions for installation and operation, from *L'Ameublement*, c. 1890.

2 The deeply recessed windows in this late 19th-century sitting room are screened with red silk shades hung outside the alcoves.

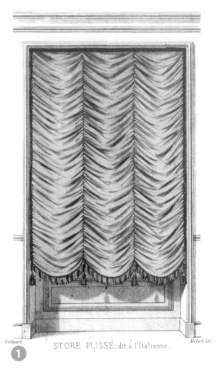

STORE PLISSÉ, dit à l'Italienne.

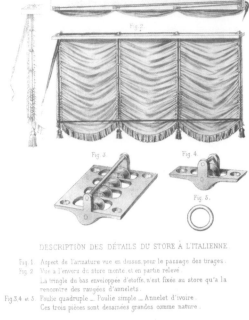

DESCRIPTION DES DÉTAILS DU STORE À L'ITALIENNE.

Fig. 1. Aspect de l'armature vue en dessus, pour le passage des tirages.
Fig. 2. Vue à l'envers du store monté, et en partie relevé
La tringle du bas enveloppée d'etoffe, n'est fixée au store qu'à la rencontre des rangées d'annelets.
Fig. 3, 4 et 5. Poulie quadruple — Poulie simple — Annelet d'ivoire.
Ces trois pièces sont dessinées grandes comme nature.

Publié par D. GUILMARD-Rue de Lancry, 2. Paris.

3 A design dating from the 1920s shows neat off-white shades in combination with a fabric valance and curtains.

4 Yellow shades make a vivid contrast with pink curtains in a late 1950s living room.

5 A graphic brown and beige print jazzes up 1970s' kitchen roller shades.

6 Shades, draperies, and wallpaper in the same floral print add up to the height of coordination, 1980s-style.

Shades

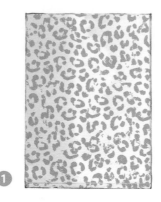

Shades

1. Pleated Roman shade

2. With bold stripes

3. With contrasting border

4. Fantail Roman shade

5. Roman shade with horizontal stiffeners sewn into the fabric

6. Soft Roman shade with side ties and tassel trim

7. With pin tucks

8. Stiffened shade with pin tucks

9. Soft Roman in sheer fabric with braid

10. Soft Roman with contrasting edging

1

2

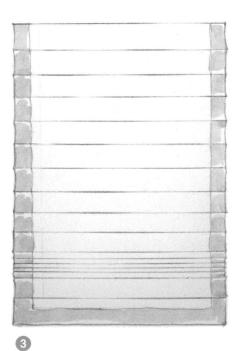

3

4

⑤

⑥

⑦

⑧

⑨

⑩

1 Single-gather shade
2 Cascade shade
3 Side-gathered shade
4 Twisted single-gather shade
5 Fan shade
6 Ruffled shade with partial Austrian gathers
7 Austrian shade
8 Austrian shade with ruffle
9 Balloon
10 Arched balloon
11 Balloon-tailed shade
12 Cloud shade
13 Ruffled cloud shade
14 Tiered cloud shade

1

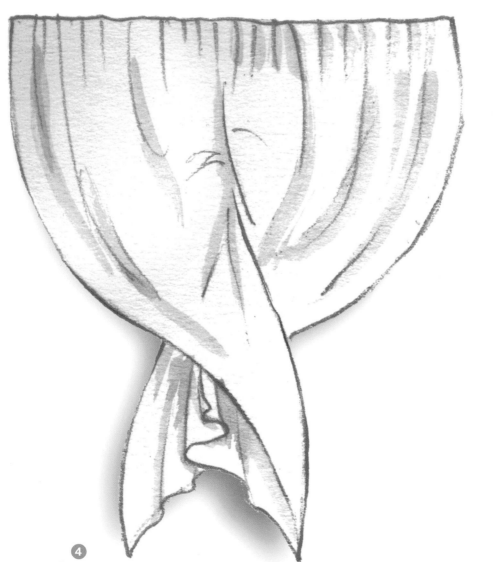

4

2

3

5

6

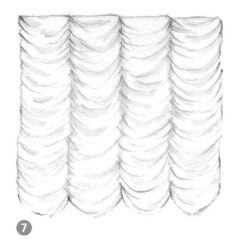

7

8

9

10

11

12

13

14

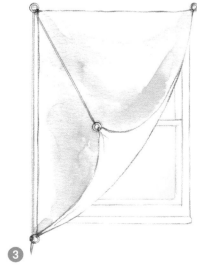

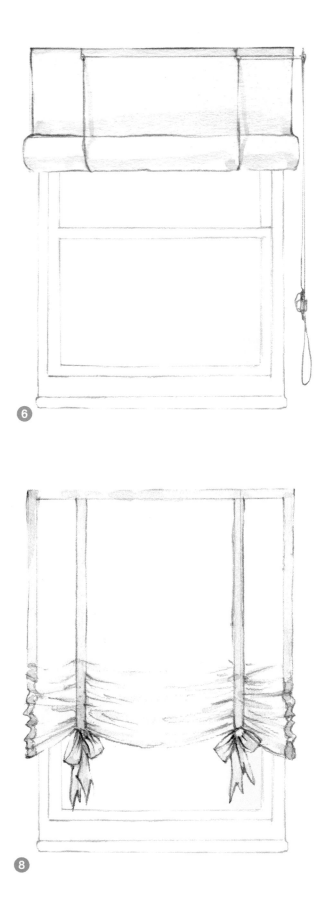

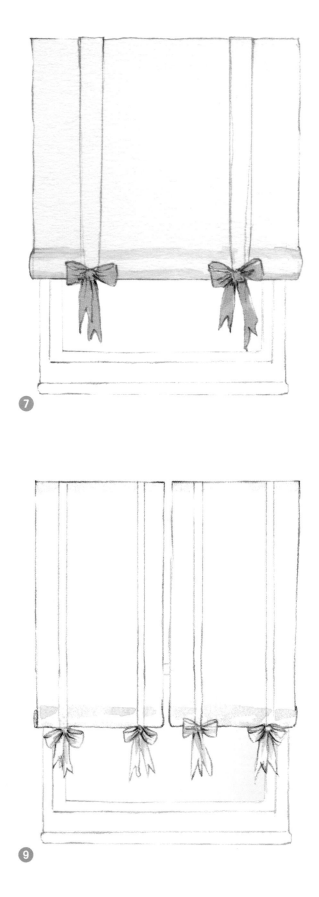

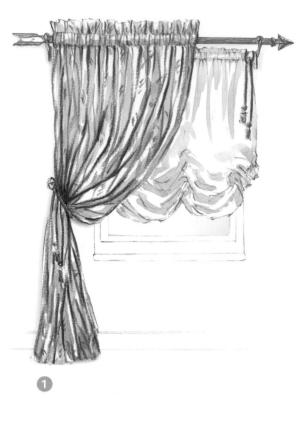

1 Silk cloud shade with toning rod-pocket tieback

2 Stiffened Roman shade in crewelwork with puddled cotton tieback panels

3 Striped Roman shade teamed with tented draperies, with foldover heading and lining in a matching fabric

4 Shaped cornice box and heavy puddled draperies, with a floral Roman shade in the same print as the fabric-covered holdbacks

5 Printed roller shade with Italian-strung draperies hung over an invisible shaped cornice

6 Central roller shade and rod-pocket tiebacks

3

4

5

6

Shades

1 Striped Roman shades at a bay window

2 Cloud shade over two sheer roller shades

3 Side-gathered shade over a long, narrow window

4 Stiffened Roman shade over two roller shades

5 Cloud shade over sheer rod-pocket panel shades

6 Roller shade in a contemporary print

7 Austrian shade over a matching roller shade

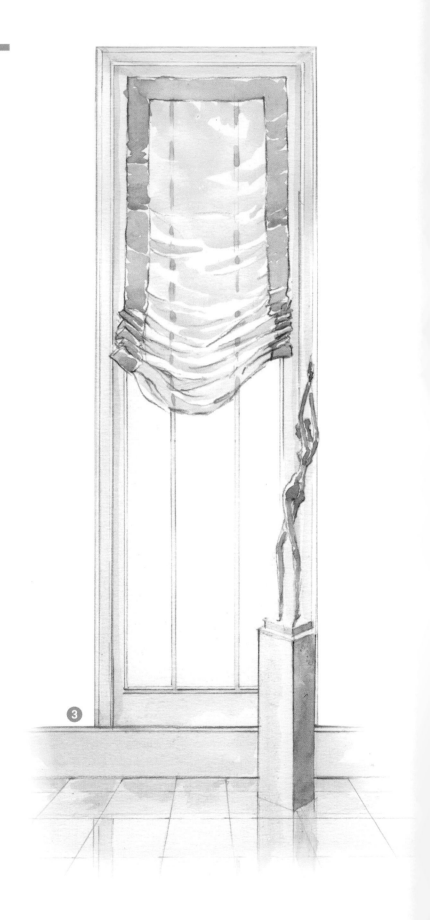

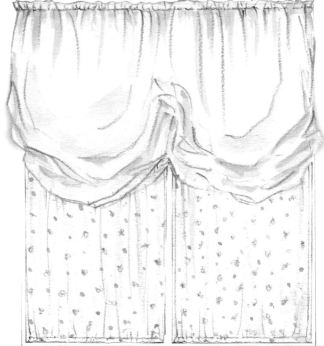

4

5

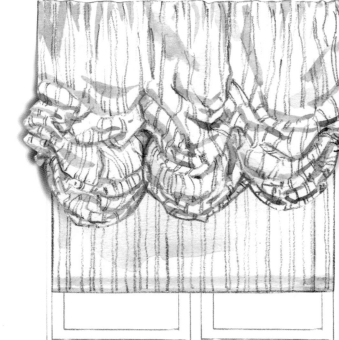

6

7

Blinds and Shutters

What distinguishes blinds and shutters from shades is, first, that blinds and shutters tend to have slats or louvers and, second, that they are generally made out of hard or stiff materials, such as wood, metal, or vinyl. The more substantial range of materials, along with the rectilinear format, means that these treatments have a more architectural look than that of curtains and shades.

Opposite Informal narrow-slatted wooden blinds provide privacy in an airy bedroom.

Above Simple horizontal louver blinds are ideal for flexible light control.

Blinds are often used in hot climates to filter strong light but let air circulate. Their offer of privacy without total loss of light is also particularly useful in urban areas. Blinds may be hung either vertically or horizontally. By adjusting the angle of the slats, light and views can be controlled precisely.

The most common type of blind is the Venetian. Its slats come in a range of widths from very narrow to several inches wide. Materials include aluminum, wood, and vinyl, and there is a considerable color and textural choice. Vertical blinds make a good choice for large picture windows or sliding glass doors. These tend to be made of stiffened fabric. Both Venetians and vertical blinds are available in stock sizes, which is less expensive than going the custom-made route. Other types of blinds include simple options made of split wood or the fancier battery-operated versions. All blinds can pose a problem with maintenance as dust collects readily along the slats, but some types can be easily taken down for washing.

Shutters are the most permanent and substantial of window treatments. They are often hinged to open like a pair of doors but may also be fixed. Depending on the type and size of the window, shutters can be installed so that they cover the window frame or are set inside it. Many shutters feature louvers that can be adjusted like the slats of a blind. Wood is a common material and may be left in a natural finish or painted to match the window frame.

With their crisp detailing, blinds and shutters suit the clean lines of contemporary interiors. They are available in a wide range of materials and formats and can be tailored to fit windows of different sizes and types. A particular advantage of this type of window treatment is variable light control. Slatted or louvered blinds and shutters allow you to adjust the degree of light a room receives while still maintaining an element of privacy. The striped patterns of light and shade are also very appealing and add vitality to the interior.

1 Horizontal fabric louver blinds for warmth as well as practicality

2 Stark slatted blinds for a striking modern look

3 Custom-designed bifold shutters made of hardwood

4 Natural wood blinds as a handsome treatment for tall windows, complementing the exposed wooden frames

5 Blinds with retractable cords for child safety

Blinds and shutters work well in many different locations and with a range of window types. Their somewhat hard-edged feel can be softened by using them in combination with draperies. Wooden blinds may be natural, painted, or stained. Aluminum and fabric blinds come in a range of colors.

1 Vertical fabric blinds for a neat and elegant way of covering large windows and glass doors

2 Horizontal fabric louvers combined with generous silk curtains

3 Louver shutters in natural oak for a sympathetic treatment in a study

4 Honeycomb blinds with electronically operated upper windows

5 Solid folding shutters painted to match the existing decoration

6 Aluminum Venetian blinds operated by remote control

177

Blinds developed as a functional way of screening strong light in the interior. Despite their modern aesthetic, blinds actually have quite a long pedigree. Venetian blinds—originally called "Persian shutters"—date back to the last quarter of the 18th century in France.

1 A 19th-century advertisement for "self-coiling steel shutters"

2 Vertical louver blinds in a 1920s Art Deco interior

3 The clean lines of blinds for a classic 1950s look

4 A 1960s advertisement demonstrating the chief advantage of blinds—adaptable light control

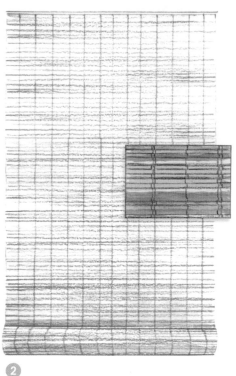

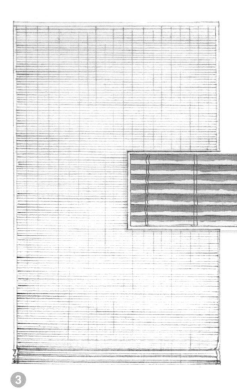

1

2

3

1 Pleated blind

2 Roll-up wooden matchstick blind

3 Woven-wood Roman-style blind

4 Venetian wood blind with tapes

5 Venetian wood blind with narrow slats and cords

6 Cellular or "honeycomb" blind

7 Vertical blind

8 A Japanese-inspired double shoji screen, made of wood with paper panels

9 A single shoji screen, blinds open

4

5

6

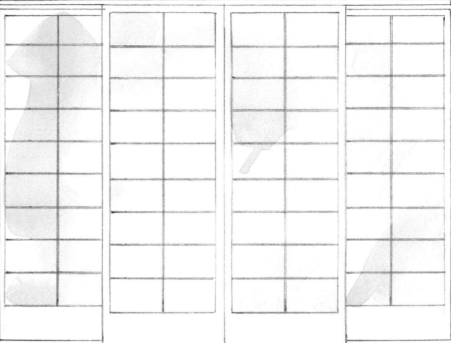

8

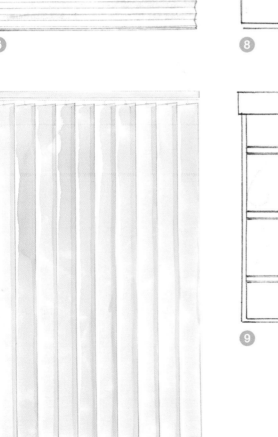

7

9

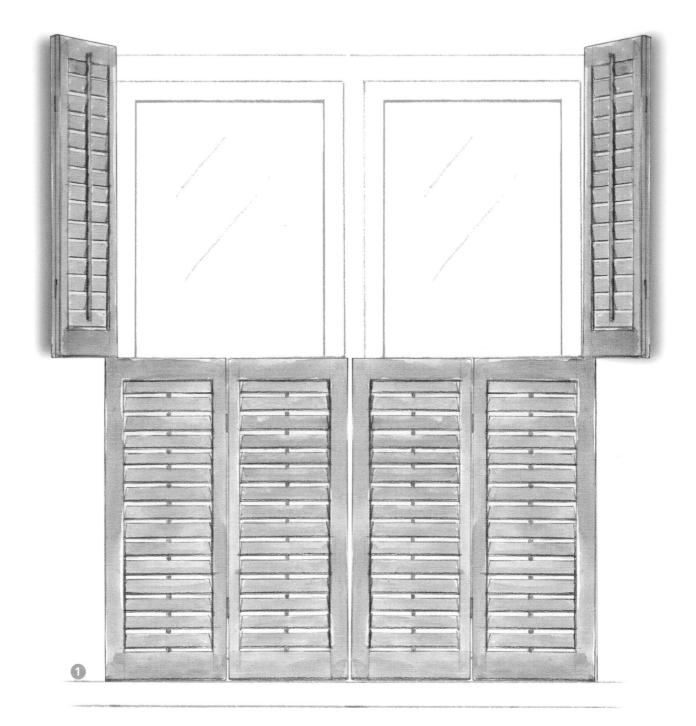

1 Natural-wood café shutters

2 Folding plantation shutters

3 Folding panel shutters

4 Plantation shutters, with adjustable slats

5 Simple shutters with fixed slats

6 A treatment for an arched window, with a central plantation shutter and a fixed blind above

7 Arched plantation shutters

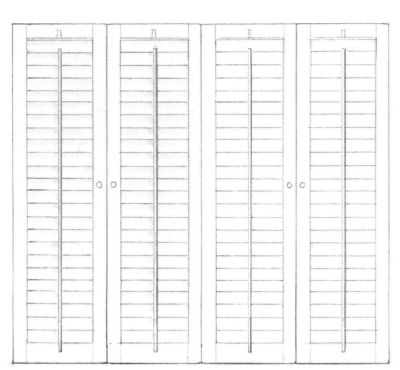

2

4

5

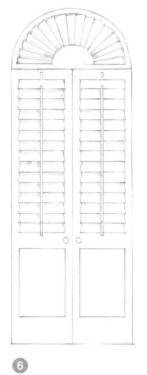

6

3

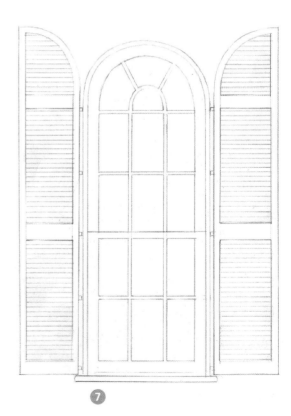

7

1 External motorized louver sunshade, made of vinyl and removeable during the winter

2 Traditional striped canvas window awning

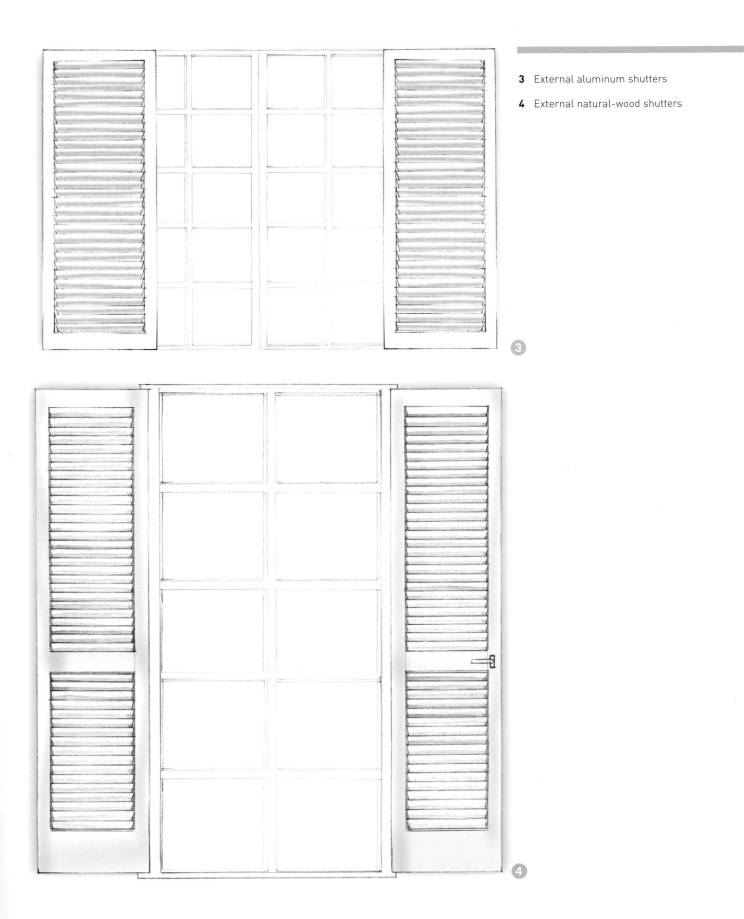

3 External aluminum shutters

4 External natural-wood shutters

1 Wooden louver blinds with a tapestry-
covered cornice box

2 Blue-painted café shutters

3 Distressed, rustic-style indoor shutters

4 Woven wood blind with a traditional
oak cornice

5 Wooden matchstick blinds with bright
fabric valances

6 Shoji screen in teak and rice paper

1 Vertical chain-linked vinyl blinds   4 Pleated sheer blinds

2 Vertical sheer blinds   5 Cellular blinds fitted to an arched window

3 Horizontal blinds with a textured pattern   6 Aluminum Venetian blinds

3

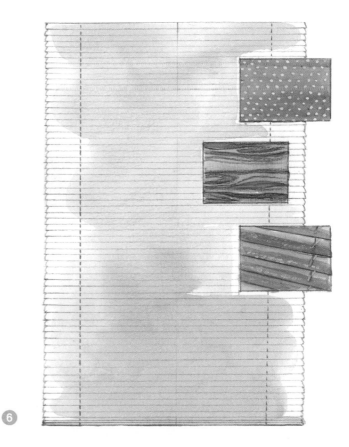

4

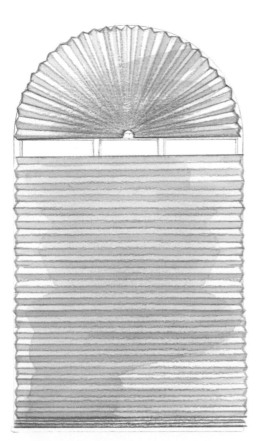

5

6

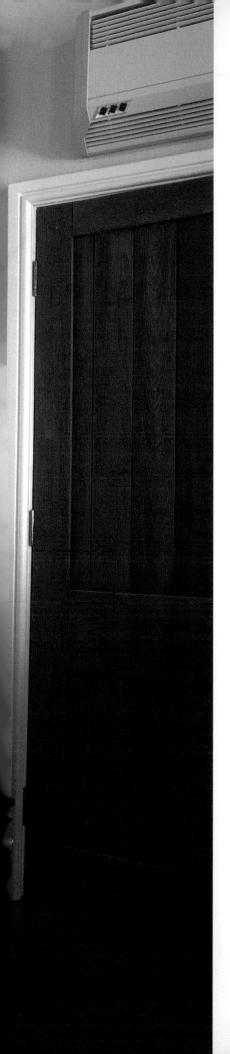

Accessories

Fabric accessories and trimmings, known as passementerie, enhance the overall style of a treatment and add extra detail to complete a look. In some cases, a trimming provides the opportunity to make a striking contrast with color or pattern; in others, it may accentuate the flowing lines of drapery or even define its shape. Trimmings are also useful ways of neatening unfinished edges.

As fabric accessories are small in scale relative to the overall window treatment, contrast of color, print, or texture is often very effective. Plain curtains can be given a graphic edge with colored or patterned trimming in the form of braid, piping, or banding. Lace edging softens crisp cotton shades; corded fringes set off the pile of velvet.

Trimming can also be used to adjust shape and proportion. The position of tiebacks, for example, will define the silhouette of curtains and hence affect the amount of light a room receives. Fringe applied to the lower edge of valances or curtains accentuates vertical lines and provides a sense of movement.

Ruffles and flounces add extra fullness to softly gathered treatments such as festoons. Accessories such as pleated fans, rosettes, and bows can be used as punctuation points, at the center of a treatment, to either side, or at the tie points of swags.

Many types of trimmings are associated with particular historical styles. Rosettes and bows, for example, were often used in the Regency period to decorate festoons and swags. Tassels and fringing are more typical of Victorian treatments. But there is no need to be restricted by tradition or convention. Trimmings and other soft accessories can be improvised from a wide range of materials to give a window treatment a whole new contemporary twist.

A tightly knotted tasseled cord used as a tieback emphasizes the fullness of heavy floor-length draperies.

191

1

Passementerie can make even the simplest window treatment look well considered, lending an accent of color, or even a touch of humor, that lifts the entire effect out of the ordinary. Where window treatments are themselves elaborate, accessories and trimmings are the icing on the cake, serving to heighten the sense of luxury.

1 A fabric flower tieback for a charming touch to simple curtains in a little girl's bedroom

2 Simple tab-top curtains with pretty satin ribbons in pastel shades

3 An added touch of color with a corded tassel tieback

4 Broad bands of contrasting edging accentuating the vertical folds of flowing panels

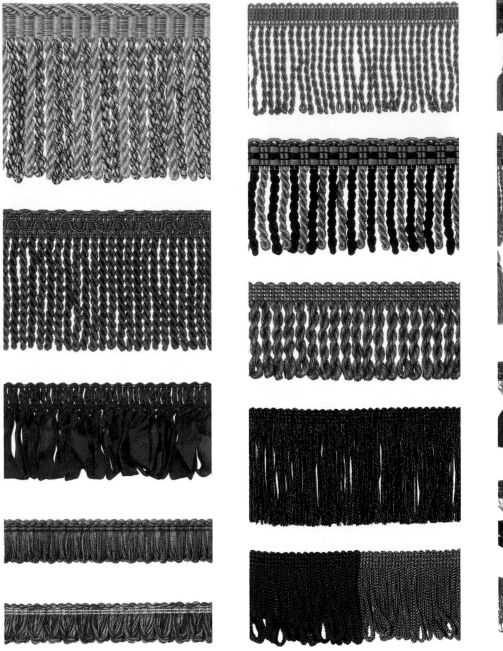

Trimmings such as tassels and fringes, composed of many individual strands, bring a liveliness and sense of movement to window treatments. Fringes range from short, brush-like edging to thick bullion fringes made of twisted cord. Many types of fringe incorporate small tassels. Fringes are inherently opulent and complement period-style effects.

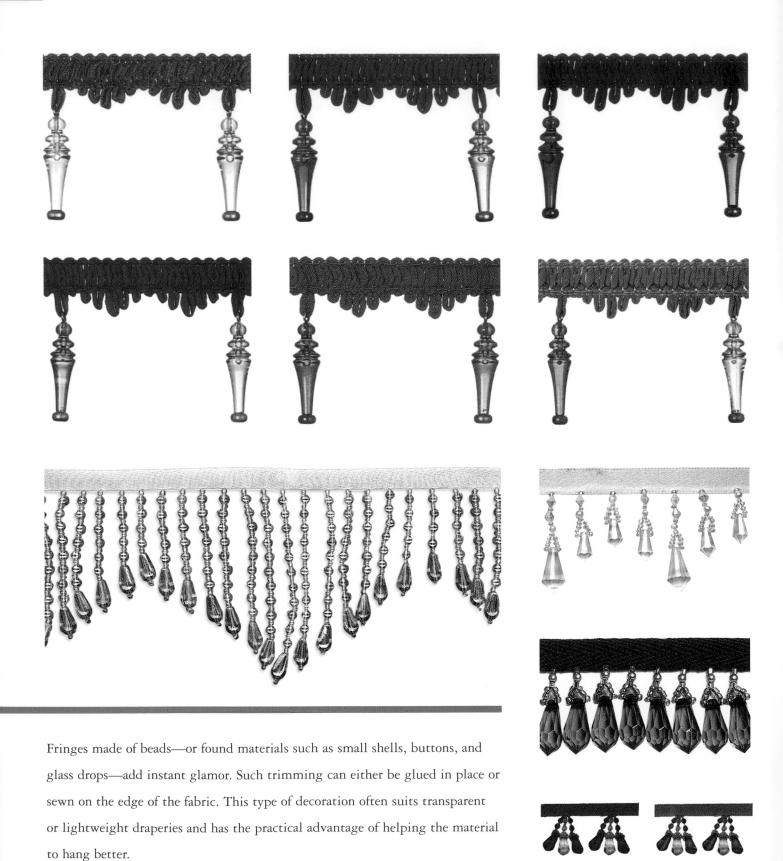

Fringes made of beads—or found materials such as small shells, buttons, and glass drops—add instant glamor. Such trimming can either be glued in place or sewn on the edge of the fabric. This type of decoration often suits transparent or lightweight draperies and has the practical advantage of helping the material to hang better.

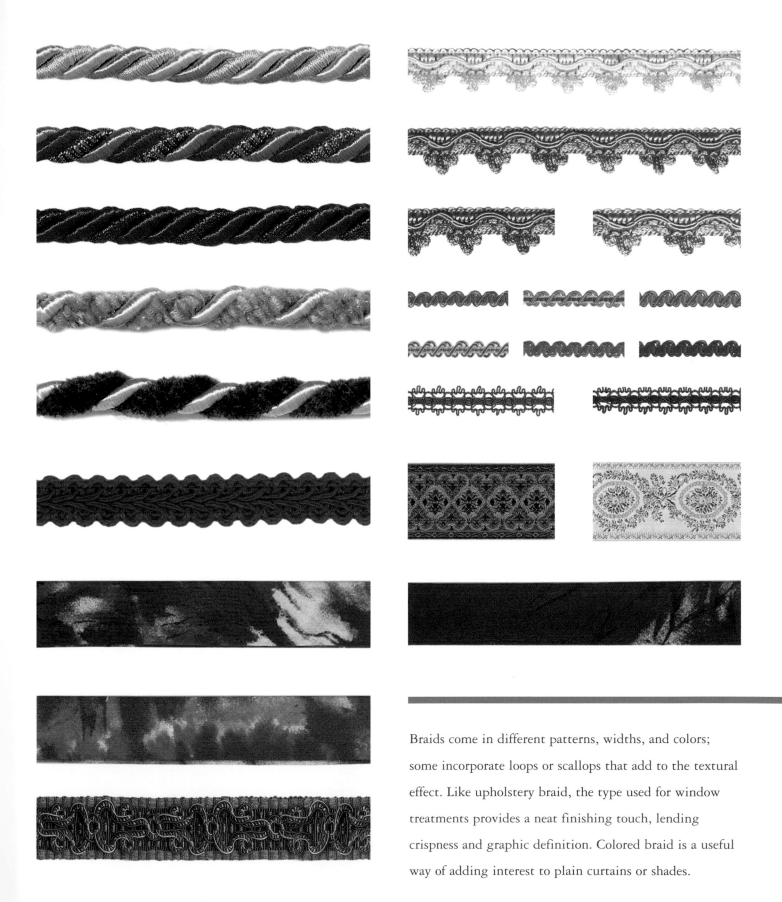

Braids come in different patterns, widths, and colors; some incorporate loops or scallops that add to the textural effect. Like upholstery braid, the type used for window treatments provides a neat finishing touch, lending crispness and graphic definition. Colored braid is a useful way of adding interest to plain curtains or shades.

Tassels are the punctuation points of window treatments and tend to be used in combination with corded ropes to serve as tiebacks. They come in a huge range of sizes and styles and are often made of silk.

Rosettes and bows, associated with French Empire-style draperies, are most commonly used to decorate the ends of top treatments, such as the places where swags meet jabots. Rosettes require sewing skills, unlike bows, which are easier to improvise. Fabric tiebacks are typically attached to small hooks on the window frame. They may be shaped, trimmed, fringed, or tasseled. In terms of color and pattern, you can opt for a bold contrast or a coordinating effect. In order for the tieback to hold its shape, it is usually stiffened with buckram and lined. Less formally, a length of fabric or a wide ribbon can serve as a simple tieback.

1	Rosette	**16**	Rounded-end tieback	**30**	Ruffled tieback
2	Knife-pleated rosette	**17**	Scalloped-edge tieback	**31**	Plain tieback with single box pleat
3	Tiered rosette	**18**	Braided-edge tieback	**32**	With multiple pleats
4	Ruffle rosette	**19**	Fringed tieback		
5	Choux (cauliflower)	**20**	Tieback with knife-pleated rosette detail		
6	Flower rosette	**21**	Plaited tieback		
7	Trefoil	**22**	Shirred tieback		
8	Maltese cross	**23**	Shirred tieback with edging		
9	Contrast-bound Maltese cross	**24**	Smocked tieback		
10	Bow	**25**	Smocked tieback with edging		
11	Double bow	**26**	V-shaped tieback		
12	Bow with tails	**27**	Striped tieback		
13	Plain fabric tieback	**28**	Bow tieback		
14	Puffed tieback	**29**	Cartridge-pleated tieback		
15	Plain tieback with contrast edging				

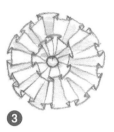

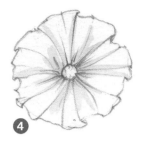

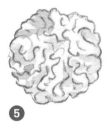

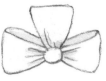

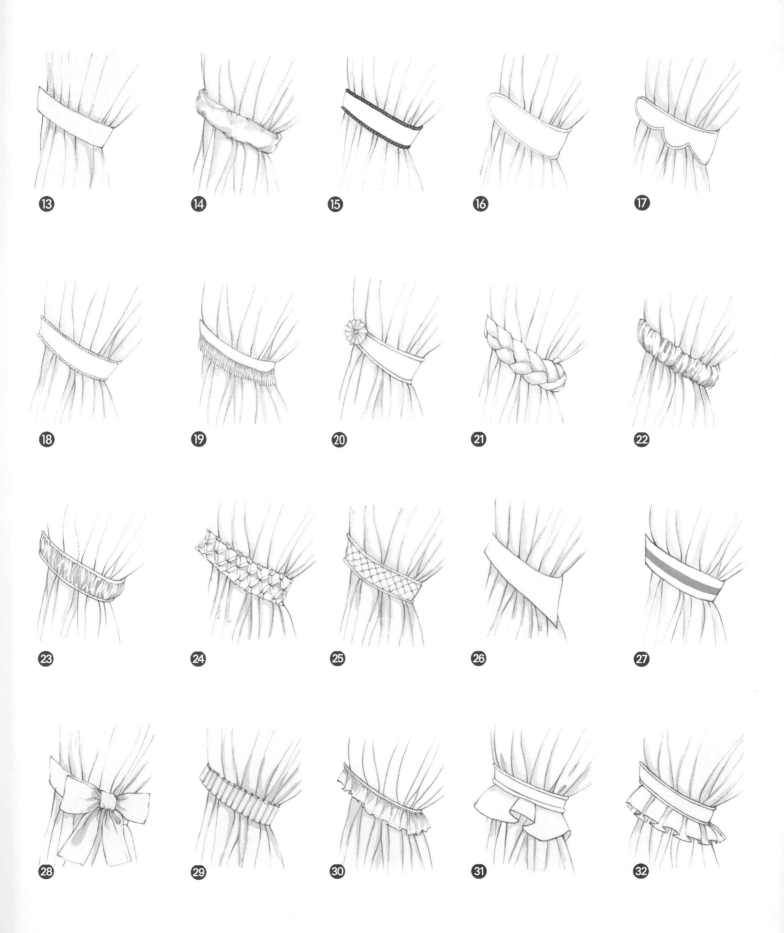

Hardware

The most important pieces of hardware are rods, poles, and tracks, which form the means of suspension for different treatments. Clips and rings allow curtains to be opened and closed. Brackets and holdbacks offer yet more decorative possibilities, while swag holders are a means of hanging a window with scarves or swags. Many types of hardware come in wooden, metal, plastic, or even stone versions.

Cheerful button-tab curtains are given a stylish lift with a wrought-iron shepherd's crook rod. The rod is fixed well above the French doors so as not to impede opening.

The big divide is between types of hardware that are essentially functional and are intended to be concealed as much as possible, and those that are decorative. Concealed rods vary widely in function; many are designed to solve specific problems. Rods that swivel allow you to curtain inward-opening casements or French doors without interference or obstruction; angled or curved rods fit inside the recess of a bay. With this type of hardware, practicality may be the sole criterion for selection.

In the case of decorative hardware, style and material broaden choice immensely. If you want decorative hardware, choose a style that complements both the window treatment itself and the architectural detailing of the room. Wooden and metal poles are widely available in a range of styles, from traditional to contemporary. Finishes also vary. Wooden poles may be stained, painted, gilded, or varnished. Rustic poles can be improvised from branches. Metal rods offer a similar range of choice, from country-style wrought iron to sleek polished chrome. Finials, which form the endpieces of rods and poles, come in a huge variety of shapes and motifs. They may be made from a contrasting material for a decorative accent.

Stylish brackets and holdbacks add a touch of grandeur to formal treatments, such as swags and full draperies. Good reproductions of historical examples are easy to find. Matching brackets and holders to finials looks well coordinated.

Where rods and poles are visible, it is important that they should be matched both to the style of the treatment and existing architectural detail. At the same time, while such hardware should complement the overall look, it should never overwhelm the treatment itself. Whatever style or material you choose, make sure that curtains can run freely along the pole or rod.

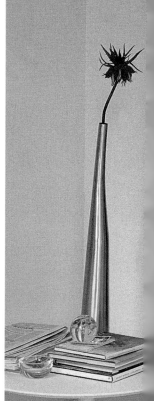

④

⑤

1 A brass leaf finial adding flair to a simple metal pole

2 A dramatic curtain treatment complemented by an elaborate pole, brackets, and holdbacks

3 Swivel rods allowing curtains to swing back from a doorway

4 Light fabric suspended from café clips threaded along a ceiling-mounted pole

5 A modern wire-and-steel double-track treatment

Hardware accessories, such as swag holders and holdbacks, make excellent finishing touches for all types of treatments, from light, filmy curtains to heavier, more tailored effects. When choosing a decorative or traditional style of accessory, it is a good idea to match it to other visible hardware, such as poles and finials.

1   Lightweight fabric simply draped over star-shaped swag holders

2   Traditional metal holdbacks positioned at sill height for a low-waisted silhouette

3   A steel-ball holdback

4   A contemporary wooden holdback

5   A holdback in the form of a metal coil

②

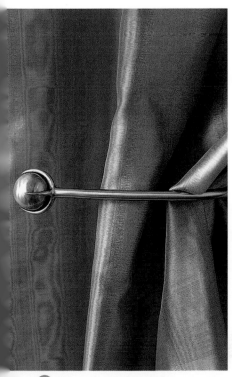

③

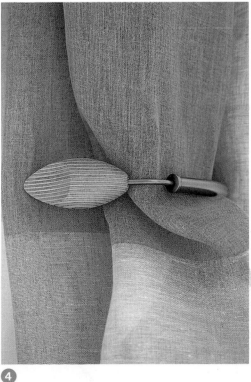

④

⑤

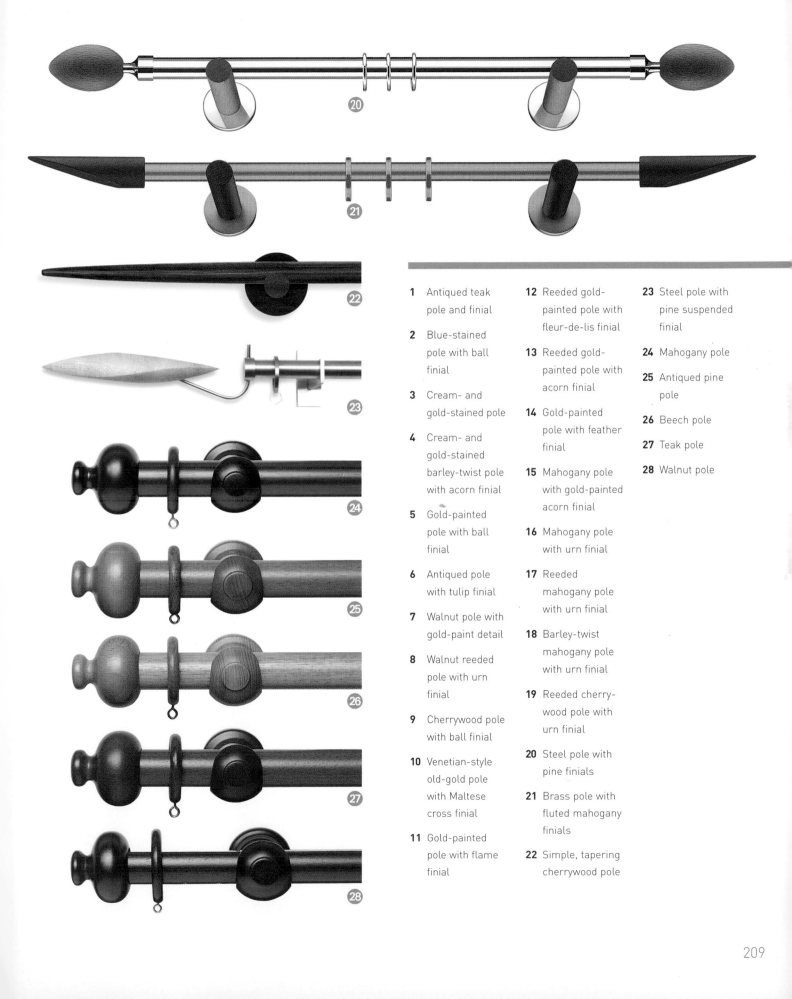

20

21

22

23

24

25

26

27

28

1 Antiqued teak pole and finial

2 Blue-stained pole with ball finial

3 Cream- and gold-stained pole

4 Cream- and gold-stained barley-twist pole with acorn finial

5 Gold-painted pole with ball finial

6 Antiqued pole with tulip finial

7 Walnut pole with gold-paint detail

8 Walnut reeded pole with urn finial

9 Cherrywood pole with ball finial

10 Venetian-style old-gold pole with Maltese cross finial

11 Gold-painted pole with flame finial

12 Reeded gold-painted pole with fleur-de-lis finial

13 Reeded gold-painted pole with acorn finial

14 Gold-painted pole with feather finial

15 Mahogany pole with gold-painted acorn finial

16 Mahogany pole with urn finial

17 Reeded mahogany pole with urn finial

18 Barley-twist mahogany pole with urn finial

19 Reeded cherry-wood pole with urn finial

20 Steel pole with pine finials

21 Brass pole with fluted mahogany finials

22 Simple, tapering cherrywood pole

23 Steel pole with pine suspended finial

24 Mahogany pole

25 Antiqued pine pole

26 Beech pole

27 Teak pole

28 Walnut pole

1 Iron fleur-de-lis finial	**8** Antiqued curlicue finial	**14** Golden pole with bud finial	**20** Steel-and-brass geometric finial
2 Iron cage-and-ball finial	**9** Brass barley-twist pole and urn finial	**15** Aluminum fleur-de-lis finial	**21** Brass arrow finial
3 Tapering iron pole	**10** Brass reeded pole and acorn finial	**16** Brass shepherd's crook finial	**22** Golden arrow finial
4 Curved iron pole with box end	**11** Brass pole and finial	**17** Venetian-style antiqued foliage finial	**23** Golden ball finial
5 Iron shepherd's crook finial	**12** Wooden pole with curled iron finial	**18** Medieval-style finial	**24** Blunt-ended steel finial
6 Wooden pole with iron ram's horn finial	**13** Double steel pole with bullet finials	**19** Wooden pole with brass arrow finial	**25** Fluted-steel finial with plastic inset
7 Spanish-style antiqued pole and finial			

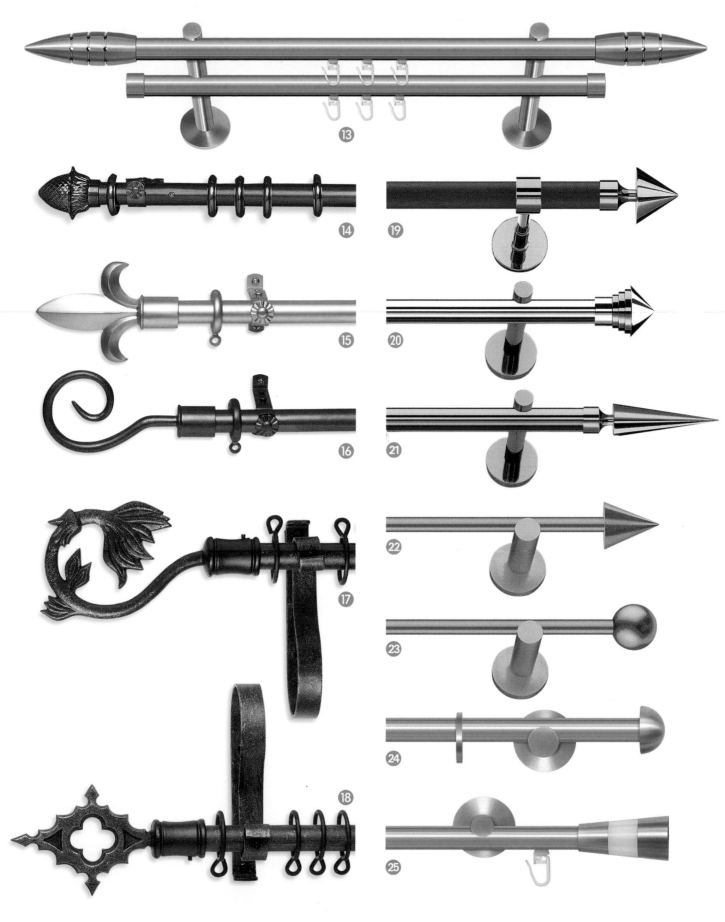

13

14   19

15   20

16   21

17   22

      23

18   24

      25

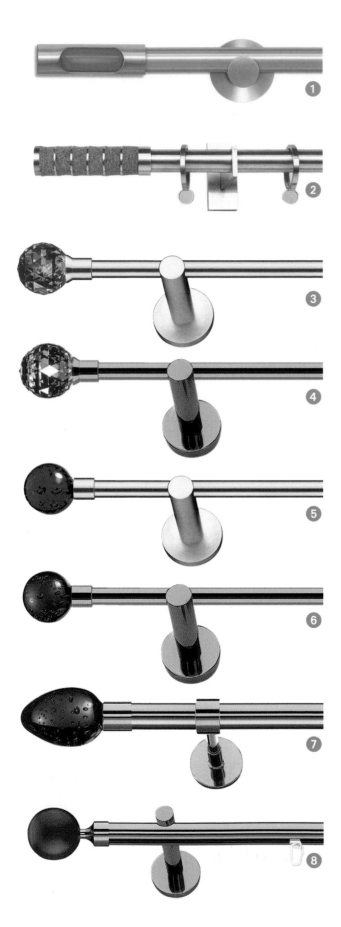

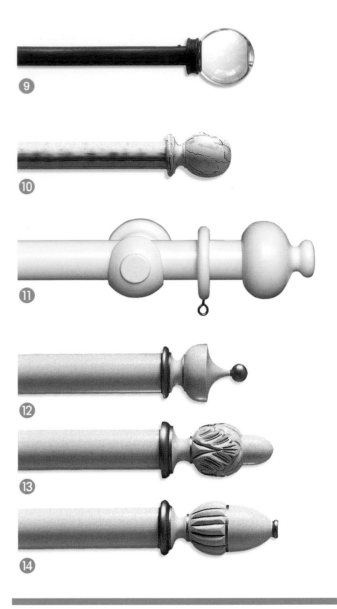

1	Steel finial with blue-glass inset	7	Brass pole with egg-shaped glass finial		finial and gold details
2	Steel pole with felt-wrapped finial	8	Brass pole with amber frosted-glass finial	13	Antiqued plastic pole with artichoke finial
3	Steel pole with blue-crystal finial	9	Iron pole with glass finial	14	Antiqued plastic pole with acorn finial
4	Brass pole with green finial	10	Faux-marble finial		
5	Steel pole with blue-glass finial	11	White plastic pole and finial		
6	Brass pole with green-glass finial	12	Cream plastic pole with urn		

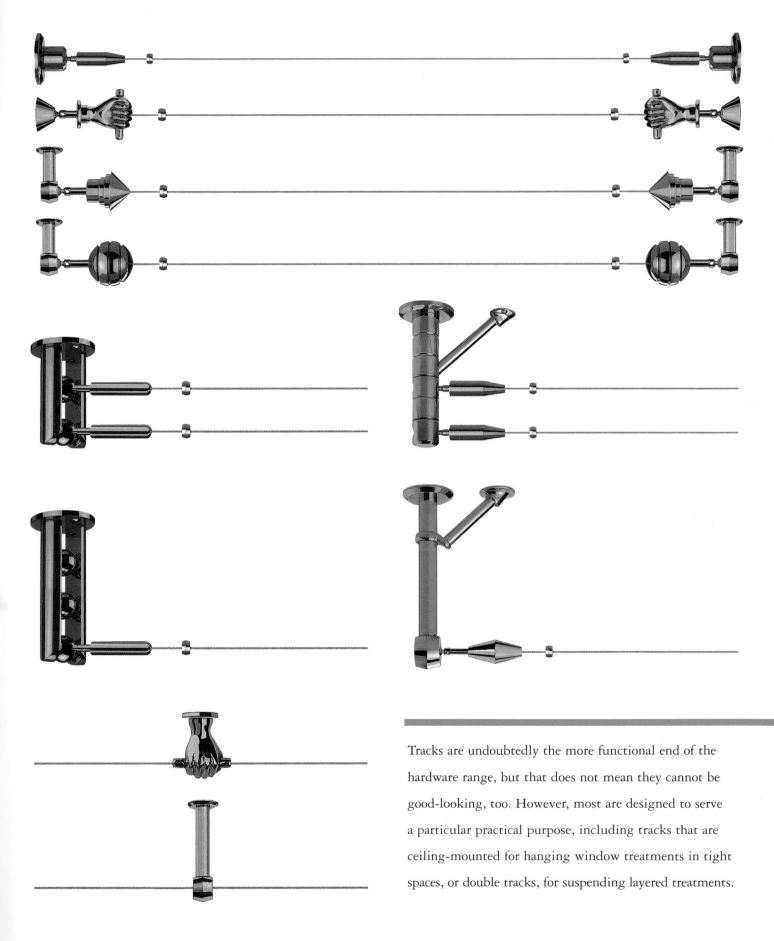

Tracks are undoubtedly the more functional end of the hardware range, but that does not mean they cannot be good-looking, too. However, most are designed to serve a particular practical purpose, including tracks that are ceiling-mounted for hanging window treatments in tight spaces, or double tracks, for suspending layered treatments.

Brackets are the means by which decorative poles are supported. They fix either to the window frame or the wall. If you choose an ornate bracket, finials should be simpler to avoid a clash of styles.

1 Oak acanthus scroll bracket

2 Plain oak bracket

3 Scroll bracket

4 Ring oak bracket

5 Fleur-de-lis oak bracket

6 Iron ring bracket

7 Iron screw bracket

8 Steel bracket

9 Unscrewable steel central bracket

10 Brass bracket

11 Steel bracket

12 Brass double bracket

13 Brass double ring bracket

The most common means of connecting curtains to a pole is rings. Rings often have a clip for grabbing the fabric directly; alternatively they may have a small ring for holding a hook attached to the fabric panel. Another means of suspension is hooks, which attach directly to the ceiling or wall and can be used with stationary curtains sewn with loops. Curtain pins are used to fasten very lightweight fabric in place in a swag or tieback.

1 Sun hook	**8** Rose curtain pin	**14** Clip ring
2 Star hook	**9** Star curtain pin	**15** Brass clip ring
3 Fleur-de-lis hook	**10** Nightingale curtain pin	**16** Brass and steel curtain rings
4 Heart hooks	**11** Eagle curtain pin	**17** Large wooden curtain rings
5 Curlicued hook	**12** Man-in-the-moon curtain pin	
6 Simple hook	**13** Sun curtain pin	
7 Brass hooks of differing sizes		

Holdbacks and swag holders are somewhat interchangeable. For example, a holdback fixed at the top of the window frame can be used for simple scarf treatments. The most common forms of holdback are knobs and loops. A holdback may also serve as a hook for a fabric or rope tieback. Consider the height at which you install the holdback, as this will greatly affect the silhouette of the window treatment. All holdbacks should be positioned so that they are hidden by the fabric panels when the curtains are closed. Many swag holders are similar to holdbacks in design, but there are more complex versions that allow you to form rosettes at the tie points of the swags.

1	Golden sun-motif holdback	**14**	Spanish-style holdback
2	Golden flower-motif holdback	**15**	Medieval-style iron holdback
3	Pine holdback	**16**	Steel shepherd's crook holdback
4	Oak holdback	**17**	Fleur-de-lis holdback
5	Gold-painted holdback	**18**	Cage-and-ball holdback
6	Limed oak holdback	**19**	Simple brass holdback
7	Beech holdback	**20**	Golden hook holdback for a tieback
8	Walnut holdback	**21**	Ball-ended hook holdback
9	Iron holdback	**22**	Brass scarf ring
10	Antiqued rose holdback	**23**	Plastic swag holder
11	Venetian-style iron holdback	**24**	Coiled scarf holder
12	Twisted-foliage holdback		
13	Medieval-style holdback		

11

12

13

14

15

16

17

18

19

20

21

22

23

24

217

Window Treatment Templates

The following templates are a great way of seeing how different styles combine with each other on a particular window. Try photocopying, enlarging, and coloring them, then mix and match until you find a look you like.

Double-hung and casement windows

1 Double-hung window

2 Casement window

3 Single tieback

4 Tab-top valance

5 Arched valance

6 Scalloped cornice

7 Draped scarf

8 Single swag

9 Centered tieback

10 Triple scarf

11 Café curtain

12 Puddled curtains

13 Rope-loop curtains

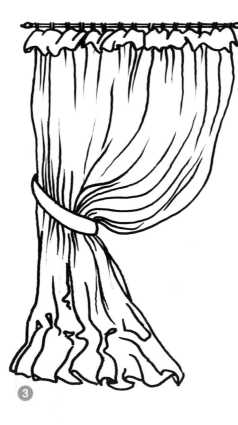

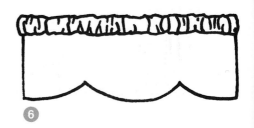

Double-hung and casement windows continued

1 Scalloped roller shade

2 Roman shade

3 Tailed balloon shade

4 Pleated blind

5 Plantation shutters

6 Café shutters

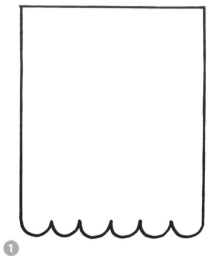

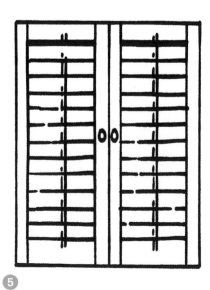

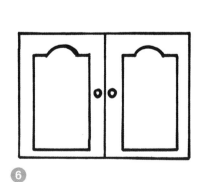

Arched windows

1 Arched window

2 Tab-top curtains hung below the arch

3 Arched blinds

4 Swag with raised center

5 Asymmetrical curtain

6 Arched shutters

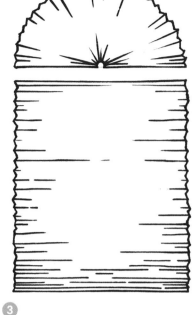

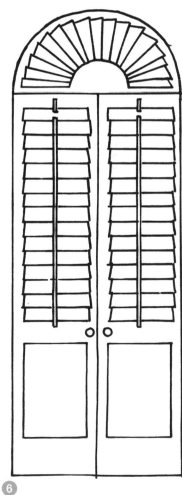

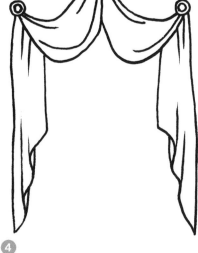

Picture windows

1 Picture window

2 Folding shutters

3 Floor-length curtains

4 Austrian valance

5 Beehive cornice

6 Traditionally shaped cornice

7 Gathered valance

8 Multiple swag and jabots

9 Plain roller shade

10 Multiple overlapping swag

11 Sill-length tiebacks

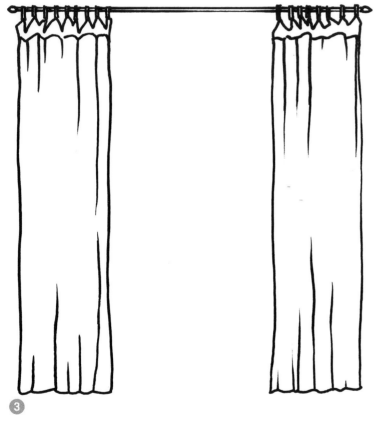

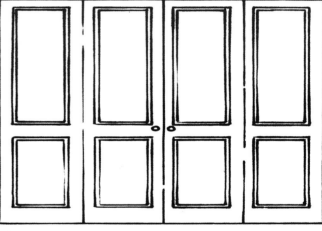

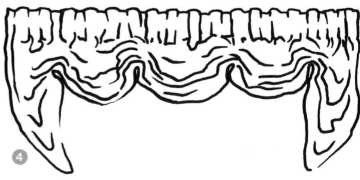

⑤

⑥

⑦

⑧

⑨

⑩

⑪

Bay windows

1 Bay window

2 Rod-pocket curtains

3 Italian-strung draperies

4 Scarf with rosettes

5 Matchstick blinds

6 Valances

7 Roman shades

8 Foldover curtains across the alcove

9 Tiebacks with valance across the alcove

1

2

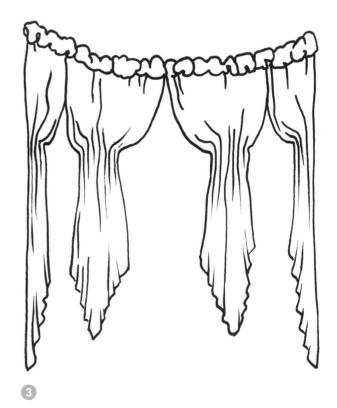

3

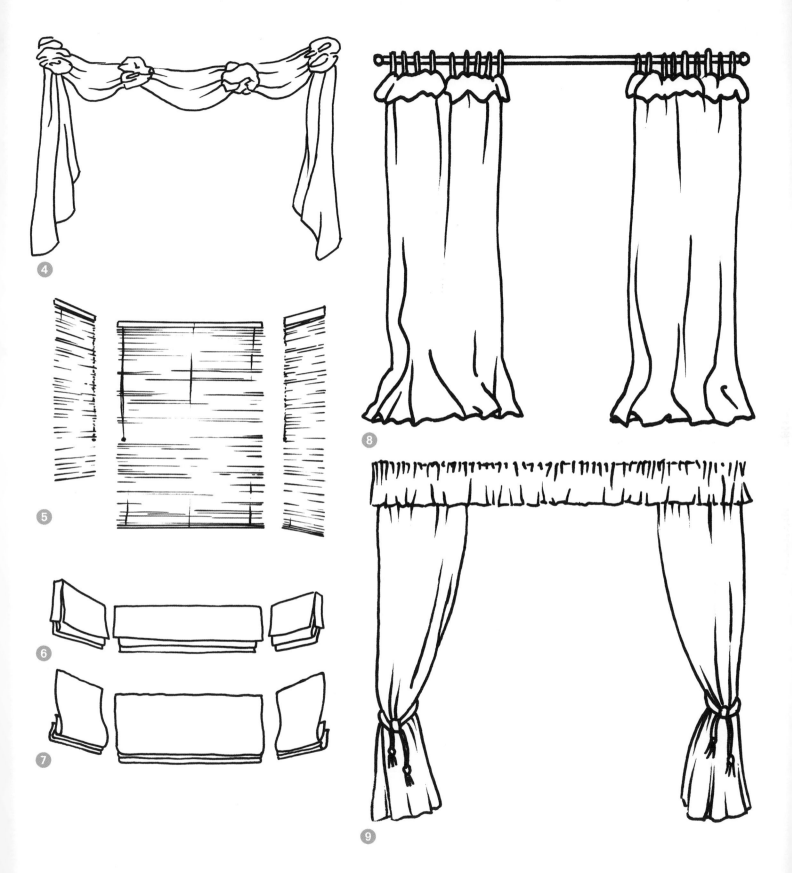

4

5

6

7

8

9

Sliding and French doors

1 Sliding doors
2 French doors
3 Banner valance
4 Turban swag
5 Roman shades

6 Shaped cornice with braid
7 Foldover tiebacks
8 Asymmetrical tieback
9 Floor-length curtains
10 Asymmetrical scarf

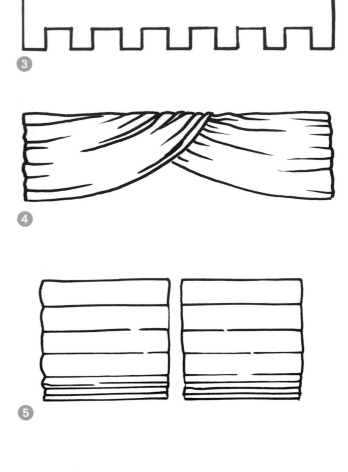

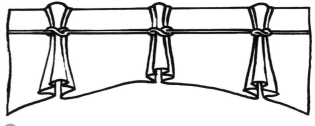

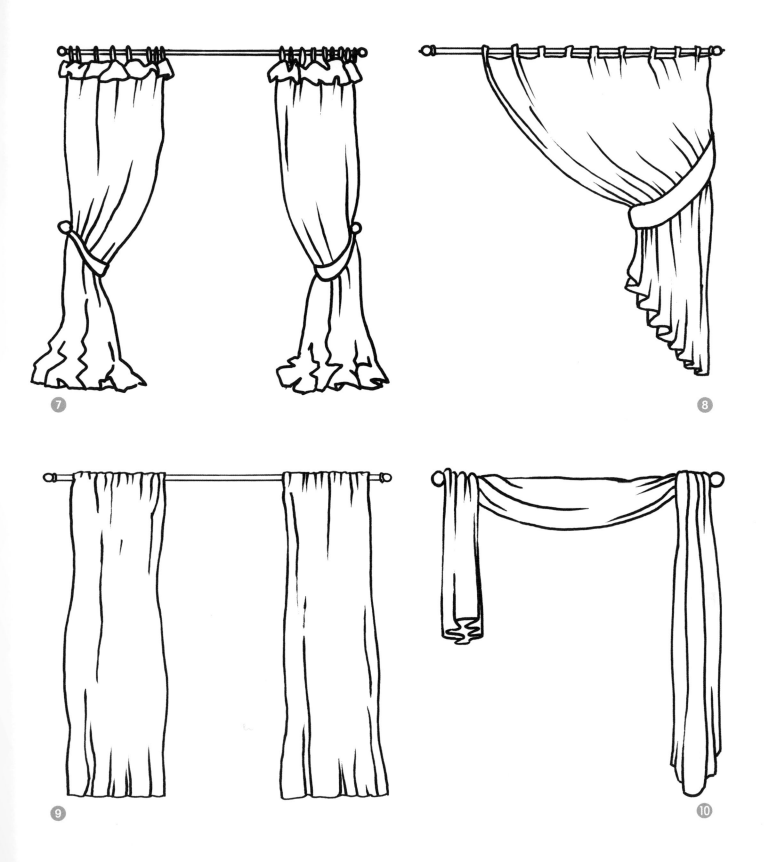

Practical Checklist

❶ Choosing fabric

Different types of fabric lend themselves to different applications, depending on type of fiber, weight, and weave. Before you buy, consider the following pointers:

• Check what the fabric is made of. Is it prone to shrinkage? Is it stain-resistant or fire-retardant? Does it require dry cleaning or can it be machine-washed? Will it fade in sunlight? Will it crease too easily?

• Roll out a length to assess the impact of color and pattern. Small swatches can be misleading. Try to view the fabric in natural light to gain an idea of true color values. Hold translucent or lace fabrics up to the light to assess sheerness and pattern, if any.

• Gather or pleat the fabric in your hands to assess the effect of different types of heading on the pattern and weave.

• Make sure you buy enough fabric to finish the job. Colors may vary from batch to batch, which could make subsequent matching difficult.

❷ Measuring windows

Whether you are making a treatment yourself or commissioning a professional to make it for you, accurate measurements are essential. Try working to the following guidelines:

• Equip yourself with a steel tape measure. Don't use cloth tapes, because they stretch out of shape and are not accurate.

• Enlist a helper, particularly if you are measuring windows that are very tall or very wide.

• Take all measurements at least twice.

• If you are measuring a pair of windows, don't assume they are the same size. Measure each one individually.

• For treatments that will hang inside the window frame or recess, bear in mind that windows are not always plumb. Measure the width at the top, middle, and bottom of the window, and choose the narrowest measure as the final width.

• For treatments that will hang outside the frame, allow for two inches' clearance to either side. For curtains, add extra inches depending on how much you would like your panels to overhang the window. If you want curtains to overlap in the middle, allow for an extra three inches' width to each panel.

• When joining patterned fabric widths, measure the distance between the beginning of one motif and the beginning of the next and add that measurement to the width you allow for each piece of fabric.

FABRIC AND FIBER TYPES

Fabric	Usage	Care
Acetate An artificial fiber with similar qualities to silk, but less likely to rot or fade	Soft draperies or any stand-in for silk	Dry clean and cool iron
Brocade Woven fabric with a raised (jacquard) design and opulent appearance; may be made of silk, wool, cotton, or blends	Draperies and top treatments	According to fiber content
Broderie anglaise Cotton fabric with pierced eyelet designs and embroidery; may shrink	Café curtains or trimming	Machine-wash cold and tumble-dry low
Cambric Closely woven cotton or linen, with a sheen on one side	Curtains	According to fiber content
Canvas A coarse cotton or cotton-and-linen blend, which comes in different weights; may shrink	Shades	Machine-wash cold and tumble-dry low
Chintz Traditional cotton fabric, typically printed with floral patterns or birds; unglazed chintz is called cretonne; glazed chintz has a resin coating on one side, giving a soft sheen and repelling dust	Curtains, draperies, and top treatments	Dry clean
Cotton A versatile fiber that may be finished in different ways or blended with artificial fibers; may be colorfast, but crumples; cotton duck is a heavy weave and may be used for no-sew curtains; cotton lawn is smooth and fine	Curtains, shades, and top treatments, depending on weight and finish	Machine-wash cold and tumble-dry low; check label for blends and care accordingly
Damask Woven fabric with jacquard design, similar to brocade but smoother and reversible; may be silk, linen, cotton, rayon, or blends	Draperies and top treatments	According to fiber content
Dotted Swiss Sheer fabric with raised or opaque dots	Sheers or under curtains	According to fiber content
Dupioni Originally imported Indian silk, now often made from viscose and acetate; textured and lightweight; may fade	Curtains, draperies, shades, and top treatments	Dry clean
Gingham Inexpensive, fresh cotton fabric with a checkered pattern of a single color on white	Mixed treatments or curtains in informal settings	As for cotton
Holland Medium-weight fabric in cotton or linen; may be stiffened; does not fray or fade	Valances and roller shades	According to fiber content
Lace Delicate openwork fabric, traditionally handmade from linen threads; handmade or heirloom lace is very expensive; machine-made lace in cotton or blends is more affordable	Sheers, panel shades, or trimming	According to fiber content
Linen Natural, strong fiber made from flax; creases easily; linen union is a hard-wearing blend of linen and cotton	Curtains, draperies, and shades, particularly Roman shades	Dry clean or hand-wash and line dry
Moiré Silk fabric with a watered or wavy pattern; synthetic moiré is made of acetate; other fabrics may also have moiré patterns	Draperies	Dry clean
Muslin Light, strong, and sheer cotton fabric, usually white or off-white; very inexpensive	Sheers and shades	As for cotton
Organdy Very light, strong, sheer cotton, treated to enhance stiffness and crispness	Curtains and top treatments	Dry clean
Polyester Artificial fabric that hangs well, often used in cotton blends to reduce creasing	Curtains, shades, and top treatments	Dry clean or wash at low temperature
Sateen Strong cotton or cotton-blend fabric with a dull sheen	Linings and curtains	According to fiber content
Satin Fabric with a strong sheen on one side; silk satins were popular in Empire and Regency periods; cotton satins are more practical today	Draperies and top treatments	Dry clean
Silk The most luxurious traditional furnishing fabric, made from the fibers of silkworm cocoons; soft and strong, but expensive and rots in sunlight	Curtains, draperies, and shades if backed by lining to prolong life	Dry clean
Taffeta Stiffer form of silk or artificial silk, smooth and shiny on both sides	Draperies and top treatments	Dry clean
Ticking Striped, hardwearing cotton fabric traditionally used to cover mattresses, with narrow stripes on a white ground	Informal curtains and shades	As for cotton
Velvet Fabric with a dense, smooth pile on one side; may be made of silk, cotton, polyester, or rayon	Curtains and draperies	Dry clean
Viscose Artificial fiber with a soft sheen, often used in blends with cotton and silk	Draperies	Dry clean

• When measuring length, allow for four inches' clearance above the frame, depending on pole or hardware position and width. A thin pole, for example, will give a different length than a thicker one. If you are using a pole, calculate "drop" from the bottom of the rings. Windows are not always plumb: take two measurements from top to bottom and then use the shortest one.

• Roman blinds need extra clearance at the top. Add eight inches to the overall length.

• For below-sill-length curtains, measure to three or four inches below the sill.

• For floor-length curtains, measure to ½ inch above the floor. If you have chosen double-tracked curtains, the inner pair should be ½ inch shorter than the outer pair.

• For puddled treatments, add an extra six to eight inches to the drop.

Each curtain panel is usually composed of a number of widths sewn together. Choice of heading will affect the amount of fabric you need. This fabric width is usually expressed as a multiple of the overall width of the treatment (remember that this is the length of the rod or pole and not the actual width of the window itself):

• Standard gathered headings need one and a half to two times the width of the rod.

• Pinch pleats need two times the width of the rod.

• Cartidge pleats need two and a half times the width of the rod.

• Pencil and box pleats need two and a half to three times the width of the rod.

❸ Budgeting

Window treatments can be expensive, particularly if you opt for a high-quality fabric. Before you commit yourself to a scheme, consider the following points:

• Work out the total cost, which may include fabric (face fabric, lining, and interlining), hardware (rods, poles, and fixings), trimmings, and top treatments such as valances; or any permutation of shades, blinds, shutters, and the above. If you are choosing a custom design, add in professional fees. If you are making it yourself, cost out your time.

• Think about how long you expect the window treatment to remain in place. Do you think you might move or redecorate in the near future? If the treatment is for a child's room, will it be outgrown sooner rather than later?

• Will the treatment incur ongoing maintenance costs? Some options may require professional assistance when it comes to maintenance and cleaning.

• If your preferred option looks as if it will be too expensive, you can cut costs by choosing a less expensive fabric or material. It is often better, however, to take a sideways step and choose a more budget-conscious style of treatment rather than compromise on basic quality.

❹ Go DIY or professional?

You can choose between the following four basic options when it comes to carrying out the work:

Do it yourself

Many simple treatments are well within the capabilities of the experienced amateur. But don't be tempted if the treatment is very elaborate: you may end up wasting expensive fabric and spending more than you might have saved on fees.

Ready-made

Many straightforward curtains, blinds, shades, and shutters are available ready-made. These tend to come in standard sizes, but are less expensive than custom and virtually instant.

Consultant

If you are confident about your practical skills but need help with ideas, ask an interior decorator to come up with recommendations for styles of treatment and choice of fabric.

Custom

Interior decorators or custom workrooms will tackle the whole job from start to finish. This is the most expensive route, but may be worth it if you're after a special effect or if your windows pose particular difficulties.

❺ Hiring professionals

The same principles apply, whether you are hiring a decorator, interior design firm, curtain-maker, or other professional.

• Do your research. Personal recommendation is often the best route, so ask friends who have had similar work done for their advice. Retailers may be able to recommend a design service. Otherwise, follow up articles in magazines and newspapers, or search the internet for design associations who may have members in your area. See also "Associations," in Resource Guide, p.234.

• Shortlist a few candidates and ask to see their portfolios. Ask for references and follow up.

• Get estimates. Compare costs before deciding which professional to hire. Very low estimates are just as suspicious as very high ones. Make sure you know what the estimate includes.

• Be specific. The clearer your brief, the less chance there is of misunderstanding.

• Put it in writing. Make sure everything is down on paper, particularly if you change your mind at a later date.

Glossary

Architrave Architectural trim or molding that frames a window or doorway

Austrian shade A ruched shade that reefs up into scallops, operated by a cord system

Balloon shade A full fabric shade with inverted vertical pleats, raised and lowered by cords

Batten A thin piece of wood that slots into the base hem of a roller or Roman shade to ensure that the fabric hangs straight

Bay window A multiple window unit that forms an angled recess

Blind One of a number of solid treatments for windows, composed of slats or panels and generally made of wood, metal, or stiffened vinyl

Bow window A multiple window unit that forms a curved recess

Box pleat An evenly spaced flat-fronted pleat, composed of two folds turned inward and sewn in place

Bracket Hardware attached to the wall to support a rod or pole, ocassionally used for scarves

Bullion fringe A fringe formed of twisted loops of rope

Café curtain A curtain that covers only the bottom portion of the window

Cascade jabot An asymmetrical tail for a swag that falls in stacked pleats

Casement window A vertically hinged window

Cathedral window A window with a pointed or triangular top

Cloud shade A full, ruched shade with a pleated or gathered heading

Cornice A shallow boxlike structure, usually made of wood, mounted over the window head to conceal hardware or adjust window proportions

Curtain A relatively informal panel of fabric used to cover a window, suspended from rings or tabs or with a gathered heading. *See also Drapery*

Dormer window A vertical window that projects from the sloping plane of a roof, often in an attic, forming an alcove in the interior

Double-hung window A window that consists of two sash that slide vertically over each other to allow the circulation of air

Drapery A formal window treatment consisting of a heavy panel of fabric, often lined and full length, with a pleated heading

Dress curtain A curtain that is for decoration only and not meant to be closed. Also known as stationary drapery

Festoon shade General term for gathered fabric shades such as balloon, cloud, and Austrian

Finial The decorative endpiece for rods or poles

French pleat A three-fold pleat also known as a pinch pleat

Fringe A decorative edging made of hanging threads or tassels

Gathered heading An informal heading in which the fabric is drawn into soft folds by cords that run through a gathering tape sewn onto the reverse

Goblet pleat A heading in which the pleat is padded to form a rounded, puffed shape

Heading Any means by which fabric is gathered or pleated across the top and attached to a rod, track, or pole

Holdback Decorative hardware that holds draperies back to either side of the window

Honeycomb blind Cellular insulating blind that looks like stacked honeycombs when seen from the side

Interlining Soft opaque fabric sewn between the main drapery fabric and the lining to block light, improve hang, and enhance insulating qualities

Italian stringing A way of drawing draperies in which the heading remains fixed and the fabric is pulled backwards and forwards by the means of diagonally strung cords

Jabot The vertical tail that hangs down to either side of a swag top treatment

Jacquard A type of weave with a raised pattern, named after the Jacquard loom, which originally used punched cards to create the design

Lambrequin A cornice with shaped sides that extend at least two-thirds of the way down the length of the window

Matchstick blind A Roman or roll-up blind made of wooden sticks

Miniblind A louvered blind in which the slats are only one inch wide

Mounting board A board attached to the window frame as an invisible means of fixing top treatments

Passementerie Soft trimmings used on treatments to add decorative detail

Pipe jabot A tail for a swag that consists of a closed tube

Piping An edge trim made of fabric and sewn into a seam

Plantation shutter A horizontally louvered shutter

Repeat The distance between one motif and another in a pattern

Return The distance between the rod or pole and the wall where the brackets are fixed

Rod pocket A heading in which the fabric is turned over and sewn to form an open-ended channel into which a rod is inserted. Also known as a cased heading

Roller shade Flat shade made of fabric or vinyl operated by a spring-mounted roller

Roman shade A fabric shade that raises into horizontal folds and is operated by cords sewn on the reverse of the fabric

Scarf Uncut fabric draped through brackets or over a pole as an ornamental top treatment

Shade Any treatment made of fabric (or sometimes vinyl) that lifts or lowers against the window pane

Shoji screen Sliding or hinged panels that operate as shutters or doors, consisting of translucent panels set in a wooden frame. Originated in Japan

Stackback The space occupied by a curtain or drapery when it is fully open

Swag A scallop-shaped top treatment generally used in conjunction with jabots

Tented tieback Draperies tied back from the window in such a way as to reveal their lining

Transverse rod A rod operated by a cord and pulley

Tieback Shaped or stiffened fabric or ties used to hold curtains and draperies back from the window. Also refers to the drapery itself

Valance A top treatment made of fabric, used on its own or to hide hardware

Venetian blind A blind composed of slats that can be angled to adjust light control, often made of aluminum or wood

Vertical blind A blind consisting of vertically aligned slats

Resource Guide

The following list of manufacturers, associations, and outlets is meant to be a general guide to additional industry and product-related sources. It is not intended as a complete listing of products and manufacturers represented by the photographs in this book.

Associations

American Sewing Guild
A nonprofit organization for people who sew
Suite 510, 9660 Hillcroft
Houston, TX 77096
Tel: 713 729 3000
www.asg.org

Window Coverings Association of America
A nonprofit organization, with a dealer directory
Suite 202C, 3550 McKelvey Road
Bridgeton, MO 63044
Tel: 888 298 9222
www.wcaa.org

Blinds and Shutters

Amazing Shutters Inc.
Synthetic wood plantation shutters
Unit 10&11, 1750 Steeles Avenue W
Concord, ON L4K 2K7
Tel: 905 660 1127
www.amazingshutter.com

Aveno Window Fashions Inc.
Blinds and shades
4795 Fulton Industrial Boulevard
Atlanta, GA 30336
Tel: 404 505 1501/1 800 783 1560
www.aveno.com

Hunter Douglas Associates Inc.
Shades, blinds, and shutters
2 Park Way, Upper Saddle River
New Jersey, NJ 07458
Tel: 1 800 789 0331
www.hunterdouglas.com

Kirsch Window Fashions
Blinds, shades, and hardware
524 W. Stephenson Street
Freeport, IL 61032
Tel: 800 817 6344
www.kirsch.com

Levolor Home Fashions
Blinds and shades
4110 Premier Drive
High Point, NC 27265
Tel: 800 538 6567
www.levolor.com

Smith & Noble
Curtains, draperies, shades, blinds, and hardware
1181 California Avenue
Corona, CA 92881
Tel: 800 560 0027
www.smithandnoble.com

Talius
Blinds and shades
7401 Pacific Circle
Mississauga, ON L5T 2A4
Tel: 800 665 5553
www.talius.com

Fabric and Soft Treatments

Benartex Inc.
Original cotton fabrics
Suite 1100, 8th Floor
1359 Broadway
New York, NY 10018
Tel: 212 840 3250
www.benartex.com

J.R. Burrows & Co.
Hand-printed fabrics and lace
6 Church Street
Boston, MA 02116
Tel: 617 451 1982
www.burrows.com

Calico Corners
A wide range of fabrics and custom services
203 Gale Lane
Kennett Square, PA 19348
Tel: 800 213 6366/610 444 9700
www.calicocorners.com

Country Curtains
Fabrics, curtains, and hardware
Red Lion Inn
Stockbridge, MA 01262
Tel: 800 456 0321
www.countrycurtains.com

Croscill Home Fashions
Curtains and hardware
25th Floor
261 Fifth Avenue
New York, NY 10016
Tel: 919 683 8011
www.croscill.com

Morton, Young & Borland Ltd
Lace and madras fabrics
Newmilns
Ayrshire, KA16 9AL
Scotland
Tel: +44 1560 321210
www.myb-ltd.com

Old World Weavers
A wide range of fabrics
D&D Building
979 Third Avenue
New York, NY 10022
Tel: 212 752 9000
www.old-world-weavers.com

Romanzia
Custom-made shades and valances
655 Country Road A
P.O. Box 72
Chetek, WI 54728
Tel: 715 924 2960
www.romanzia.com

Sherwoods Fabrics Ltd
Art Nouveau fabrics
39 Church Street
Great Malvern
Worcestershire, WR14 2AA
England
Tel: +44 1684 572 379
www.sherwoodsfabrics.co.uk

Spiegel
Soft treatments, blinds, accessories, and hardware
Spiegel Customer Satisfaction
P.O. Box 6105
Rapid City, SD 57709
Tel: 800 474 5555
www.spiegel.com

Stroheim & Romann/JAB
Fabrics, trimmings, and hardware
31–11 Thomson Avenue
Long Island City, NY 11101
Tel: 718 706 7000
www.stroheim.com

Universal Draperies Inc.
Drapery fabrics
114 Advance Boulevard
Brampton, ON L6T 4J4
Tel: 800 265 5127
www.universaldraperies.com

Waverly
Fabrics and ready-made curtains
Tel: 800 423 5881
www.waverly.com

Hardware

Atlas Homewares
A wide range of hardware
326 Mira Loma Avenue
Glendale, CA 91204
Tel: 800 799 6755
www.atlashomewares.com

The Bradley Collection Ltd
A wide range of hardware
Lion Barn
Maitland Road
Needham Market
Suffolk, IP6 8NS
England
Tel: +44 845 118 7224
www.bradleycollection.co.uk

Freder Textiles
Drapery hardware and soft goods
550 Montpelier
Montreal, QB H4N 2G7
Tel: 800 361 5920
www.fredertextiles.com

Graber Window Fashions
A wide range of hardware
www.graber.ws

Hunter & Hyland
A wide range of hardware
201–5 Kingston Road
Leatherhead
Surrey, KT22 7PB
England
Tel: +44 1372 378511
www.hunterandhyland.co.uk

Integra Products Ltd
Hardware and accessories
Eastern Avenue
Lichfield
Staffordshire, WS13 7SB
England
Tel: +44 1543 267100
www.integra-products.co.uk

Ona Drapery Company
Holdbacks, rods, and finials
5320 Arapahoe Avenue
Boulder, CO 80303
Tel: 1 800 231 4025
www.onadrapery.com

Trimmings

Flecotex
Tiebacks, fringes, and braids
C/ Duquesa de Almodóvar
6–03830 Muro del Alcoy
Alicante
Spain
Tel: +34 96 654 40 32
www.flecotex@flecotex.com

Handsome Trimmings
Tiebacks and trimmings
6 Queens Square Business Park
Honley
Holmfirth, HD9 6QZ
England
Tel: +44 1484 316306
www.handsometrimmings.co.uk

Jones & Co. (Nottingham) Ltd
Hardware and accessories
Lortas Road
New Basford
Nottingham, NG5 1EH
England
Tel: +44 115 978 1263
www.jonesnottm.co.uk

Newark Dressmaker Supply and Home-Sew
Trimmings and drapery basics
P.O. Box 4099
Bethlehem, PA 18018-0099
Tel: 800 344 4739
www.homesew.com

Price & Co. (Regency) Ltd
Trimmings and hardware
Regency House
North Street
Portslade
East Sussex, BN41 1ES
England
Tel: +44 1273 439527
www.price-regency.co.uk

Rashmishree
P.O. Box 723
Pine Brook, NJ 07058
Tel: 973 808 1566
www.rashmishree.com

Sevinch
1403, 15 Hassan Sabry Street
Zamalek
Cairo 11211
Egypt
Tel: +20 2735 3439
www.passementerie.org

Index

Acknowledgments

The publishers would like to thank the following companies for their assistance:
The Bradley Collection Ltd, Büsch, Calico Corners, Country Curtains, Flecotex, Hunter Douglas Associates Inc., Hunter & Hyland, Integra Products Ltd, Jim Lawrence Traditional Ironwork Ltd, Jones & Co., Morton Young & Borland Ltd, Newark Dressmaker, Price & Co., Sevinch (photography by Michael Deman), Sherwoods Fabrics Ltd, Smith & Noble, Stroheim & Romann/JAB.

Cover photos Front Retna Back (top to bottom) Hunter Douglas, Bradley Collection, Retna, Smith & Noble
2 Retna
6 Calico Corners
7 Hunter Douglas Associates Inc.
8 Above Hunter Douglas Below Retna
9 Hunter Douglas
10 Stroheim & Romann/JAB
11 Left Retna Right Stroheim & Romann/JAB
13 Top Redcover Bottom Corbis
14–15 Hunter Douglas
38 Country Curtains
40–41 1 Hunter Douglas 2, 4 Redcover 3 Smith & Noble
42–43 1 Retna 2–3 Redcover 4 Stroheim & Romann/JAB
44–45 1–6 Corbis
46–47 1–5 Corbis
70 Redcover
72–73 1, 5 Redcover 2 Corbis 3 Country Curtains 4 Beateworks/Getty
76–77 4 Corbis
92 Integra Products Ltd
94–95 1 Hunter Douglas 2, 5 Retna 3, 6 Smith & Noble 4 Stroheim & Romann/JAB
96–97 1, 2, 4 Stroheim & Romann/JAB 3 Integra Products 5 The Bradley Collection Ltd
98–99 1 Redcover 2, 4 Bradley Collection 3 Retna 5 Stroheim & Romann/JAB
100–101 1 Sherwoods Fabrics Ltd 2, 4–8, 11, 14–16 Country Curtains 3, 9, 10, 13 Calico Corners 12, 17 Stroheim & Romann/JAB
102–103 1 (1 & 2), 3–5, 8–10 Stroheim & Romann/JAB 1 (3 & 4) Sherwoods Fabrics 2, 3, 7 Calico Corners 11–17 Country Curtains
104–105 1 (1, 3, 4), 2–7, 9, 10, 13–15, 17 Stroheim & Romann/JAB 1 (2), 8 Calico Corners 11, 12, 15 Country Curtains
106–107 1–3, 15 Stroheim & Romann/JAB 4, 5, 7, 14, 16 Calico Corners 6, 8–13, 17 Country Curtains
108–109 1, 8 Stroheim & Romann/JAB 2–7 Country Curtains 9–17 Calico Corners
110–111 1 Calico Corners 2–7, 9 Morton, Young & Borland 10–19 Country Curtains 20 Stroheim & Romann/JAB
112–113 Redcover
114–115 1 Redcover 2 Hunter Douglas 3–5 Country Curtains

116–117 1 Smith & Noble 2 Hunter Douglas 3 Country Curtains 4 Beateworks/Getty
118–119 5–6 Corbis
132 Smith & Noble
134–135 Redcover
138–139 4, 5 Corbis
150–151 Smith & Noble
152–153 1 Stroheim & Romann/JAB 2, 3, 5 Smith & Noble 4 Hunter Douglas
154–155 1, 2, 5 Smith & Noble 3, 4 Stroheim & Romann/JAB
156–157 1, 3 Smith & Noble 2, 4 Retna 5 Calico Corners
158–159 2 Corbis 3 Art Archive 4 Tony Price 5 Camera Press 6 Ad Archive
172 Smith & Noble
173 Hunter Douglas
174–175 1, 2, 3, 5 Hunter Douglas 4 Smith & Noble
176–177 1, 2, 3, 4, 6 Hunter Douglas 5 Beateworks/Getty
178–179 1, 4 Ad Archive 2 Art Archive 3 Corbis
190–191 Redcover
192–193 1 Redcover 2 Retna 3 Flecotex 4 Calico Corners
194–195 Price & Co. exc. 9, 10 Flecotex
196 1–6 Price & Co. 7–11 Newark Dressmaker
197 1–5 Flecotex 6–8, 10–13, 22–24 Newark Dressmaker 9 Sevinch (Michael Deman) 14–21 Price and Co.
198 Flecotex exc. bottom right Sevinch (Michael Deman)
199 1, 2 Price & Co. 3–13 Flecotex 14–17 Sevinch (Michael Deman)
202 Retna
204–205 1 Country Curtains 2 Integra Products 3–5 Bradley Collection
206–207 1 Beateworks/Getty 2–5 Bradley Collection
208–209 1, 5, 10, 24–28 Integra Products 2–4, 7–9, 11–19 Hunter & Hyland 6 Jones & Co. 20–22 Büsche 23 Bradley Collection
210–211 1, 2 Jim Lawrence 3–6, 12, 13, 19–25 Büsche 7, 8, 14–18 Integra Products 9–11 Hunter & Hyland
212 1, 3–8 Büsche 2 Bradley Collection 9 Jim Lawrence 10, 12–14 Hunter & Hyland 11 Integra Products
213 Büsche
214 1–5 Integra Products 6, 7, 10–13 Büsche 8, 9 Bradley Collection
215 1–13 Hunter & Hyland 14, 15, 17 Integra Products 16 Büsche
216–217 1, 2, 9, 19–21 Büsche 3, 11–18, 22, 23 Integra Products 4–8, 10 Jones & Co. 24 Jim Lawrence